Revelations of Mind

Revelations
of Mind

Tarthang Tulku

Dharma Publishing

UNDERSTANDING SELF AND MIND
*Knowledge of Freedom: Time to Change,
Revelations of Mind*

ISBN 978-0-89800-036-8
Library of Congress Control Number: 2013934207

Copyright © 2013 Dharma Publishing.

All Rights Reserved.
No part of this book may be copied, reproduced, published, distributed, or stored in any form without the express written consent of Dharma Publishing. Unauthorized reproduction is a violation of the laws of the United States and/or international copyright conventions. For more information, contact Dharma Publishing, Editorial Office, 2425 Hillside Avenue, Berkeley, CA 94704

Printed in the USA by Dharma Publishing, Ratna Ling, 35755 Hauser Bridge Road, Cazadero CA 95421

*Dedicated to the Unfolding
of Understanding*

Contents

Introduction   xv
How to Read this Book   xxv

SECTION ONE
A FRESH LOOK AT MIND   1

1	The Central Importance of Mind	2
2	Mind and I	8
3	The Business of Mind	13
4	Mind and Language	16
5	Rules for Reality	23
6	Customer Mind	3?
7	Mind on Automatic	36
8	Identifier Mind	42
9	Victimizing Mind	48
10	Dependence on Identity	56
11	Questioning the Foundation	60

Contents

SECTION TWO
WORKING WITH THE MIND — 69

12	Mirrors of Mind	70
13	Watching the Mind	73
14	Silence and Awareness	79
15	The Problem with Ownership	86
16	Getting What We Look For	90
17	Cutting Through Mind-Business	95
18	Obeying the Parameters	99
19	Closing Access to Awareness	102
20	Closed Circuitry of Mind	106
21	Understanding the Inner Story	109
22	Seeds of Separation	114
23	Validating the Validator	117
24	The Reality-Realm of Mind	122
25	Turning Toward Clarity	127

SECTION THREE
MIND AND TIME — 133

26	Time to Understand	134
27	Architect of Time	137
28	Labels and Identity	145

29	The Forward Thrust of Time	154
30	A Seeming Continuity	160
31	Opening the Nanosecond	167
32	Ground of Illusion	172
33	Sensitivity of Mind	179
34	Engine of Mind	184
35	Another Kind of Mind	189

SECTION FOUR
GROUND OF UNDERSTANDING — 195

36	Programmed Dynamic of Mind	196
37	The Knowing Mind	203
38	Re-Visioning Time and Mind	208
39	Room for Understanding	212
40	Turning to Understanding	220
41	Foundation for a New Way of Being	227
42	Recognizing Misunderstanding	231
43	Transforming Characters of Experience	236
44	Relief for the Restless Mind	241
45	Steps Toward Understanding	248
46	Imitations of Understanding	252

Contents

SECTION FIVE
LADDER OF UNDERSTANDING — 257

47	Finding the Right Track	258
48	Deactivating Dualistic Mind	262
49	Understanding Accommodates	266
50	Candidate for Understanding	271
51	Acknowledging Misunderstanding	275
52	Miracle of Understanding	282
53	Excavating Understanding	286
54	Why We Need Understanding	289
55	Ladder of Understanding	294
56	Obscurations of Mind	300
57	Gift of Understanding	305
58	A Ceaseless Unfolding	309

SECTION SIX
REVEALING UNDERSTANDING — 311

59	Tracking Back the How	312
60	How We Understand	321
61	Benefits of Understanding	326
62	Self-Mastery Through Understanding	332

Contents

63	Guidelines for Understanding	338
64	Understanding Beyond Mind and Time	341
65	Knowledge-Ability of Understanding	345
66	Freedom of Understanding	350
67	Envisioning a Regime of Understanding	353
68	Extending Understanding	357

AFTERWORD
LIGHT OF KNOWLEDGE   361

Sustaining the Light: 401
Efforts to Preserve
a 1,400-year Heritage of Wisdom

44 Years of Production: 409
Dharma Publishing Books
in Tibetan (Summary)

Dharma Publishing Books   410
in English (Summary)

Organizations and Projects   417
Established by TNMC

Introduction

We are not talking about history.

We are talking about life.

This is not our own little story

and it is not past history we are recording.

It is the way our minds are operating.

It is living history. Living experience.

Introduction

Looking back on the millennia of human history, we may marvel at how far we have come to attain our present ways of life. Over the past two hundred years alone, the age of reason and scientific exploration has opened entirely new avenues of understanding ourselves and our surroundings, from the far reaches of the universe to the microscopic realm of atoms and particles. Advances in technology and medicine continue to improve living conditions for people in many parts of the world. Each season brings new fashions, new products, new devices for communication and electronics. Even social attitudes and economic patterns, as well as occupations and lifestyles, are continuously in flux.

Yet, in fundamental ways, human beings remain much the same. As children, we are educated by parents and teachers to fit into social roles and occupations, and trained in the patterns and behaviors expected of our status and

Introduction

position. As independent adults, we exercise the views, priorities and attitudes with which we identify, while earlier influences continue to shape the fundamental orientation of our minds, manifesting in thoughts, feelings, language and emotional responses.

As in ages past, we still pursue pleasure and seek to avoid pain; we still strive to accomplish and be successful in what we do. We still follow our senses, our thoughts, and our imagination and rely upon judgments of right and wrong, good and bad that have not changed substantially throughout the course of human history. Our attitudes and views are shaped by patterns of language that have come down to us through our families and culture, and we connect sound and gestures with meaning in characteristic ways to establish our reality. We respond to the need to make ourselves acceptable to others and fit in with what has been established.

Within the established structures for thought, communication and action, there is little room to develop another understanding of reality or to generate a new vision. Even philosophers, religious leaders, artists, and other creative individuals continue to track along well-worn paths, unable radically to change the patterns of language or the rules that govern the prevailing logic. From time to time, conditions shift, clearing the way for new forms, styles and movements, but a certain continuity underlying the fabric of ordinary life inhibits even the most visionary and creative among us.

Outworn conventions may be challenged and even overturned, but fundamental assumptions go unquestioned. For example, we still see reality from the perspective of the self—the self that announces "I am" and claims ownership of everything that can be thought or perceived. As soon as we grant this sense of identity primacy in our lives, what 'I' believe, what 'I' want, what 'I' possess and what 'I' think become the operating principles of our lives.

Once the dichotomy of self and other is accepted, the logic of this assumption is automatically reflected in patterns of thought and speech. Language conveys the sense of sequential actions related to past, present, and future, reinforcing our perception that this is the way time operates. Vocabulary and grammar enable language to express the polarities of pros and cons, subject and object, pain and pleasure, and various degrees of good and bad, right and wrong. Each noun has its associations and

Introduction

connotations, each adjective expresses shadings of meaning and enables finely detailed comparisons. Shaped by syntax into interlocking units of meaning, these tightly woven patterns support a dualistic view of reality based on unquestioned distinctions of self and other. Imprinted in mind, the patterns of language become the structure of our identity and the framework of our thoughts, where they strongly influence what we accept as real and true. Expressions that do not accord with them are often dismissed as meaningless.

If we were fully attuned to the creative unfolding of each moment and all that this unfolding potentiates, our lives could manifest like chapters in a deeply engaging book; we could savor experiences while their flavors were still alive with the freshness of immediacy. Line by line, page by page, our book of life would relate a meaningful journey, satisfying in the present and rich in memories to be treasured and revisited. As one chapter closed, the next one would begin, revealing open fields to populate with new thoughts, ideas and experiences.

Yet very few individuals use their life experiences in such empowering and energizing ways. Focused on the future or sorting through memories of the past—planning, worrying, imagining

Introduction

what may or may not come about and speculating upon how best to respond to endless "what if's"—our minds are far away from the immediacy of the present. We tend not to notice what our eyes are seeing, our ears hearing, and our bodies sensing, or even what is going on in our minds. Of all that we do every day, we remember very little, and the quality of our experience is dulled by mind's lack of attentiveness. In this situation, it can be difficult to enjoy the full measure of our life experiences, and even more difficult to learn from them. This is deeply unfortunate, since the ability to learn from experience is among the most precious benefits life offers.

Our experience is more than the thoughts, emotions and events that stand out in memory. What happens when we turn our attention inward to observe and listen? Very quickly we become aware of a nearly constant mental activity that manifests as internal dialogues. We may not have paid much attention to these dialogues before, dismissing them as mind idly playing with thoughts, or as part of our efforts to think through and resolve issues that are unclear. But if we focus with awareness on this internal chatter, we may notice that mind is playing two distinct roles. One aspect of mind is noticing,

Introduction

another is listening. Further, the noticer is making statements that the listener is receiving and interpreting. There is mind that perceives, cognizes, and identifies, and mind that acts upon what has been cognized. Moving back and forth, sealing and validating cognition through recognition, mind creates the continuity it requires to sustain our view of reality.

Looking more deeply, we find that within this inner realm, many activities are in process simultaneously. There are thoughts and imagery that entertain and project as visualizations or fantasies, reflecting back to mind and stimulating imagination and trains of thought. There is a judge who assesses good and bad, right and wrong. There is a discriminator who determines what to like or dislike, what to accept and what to reject. There is the self that we express as 'I', 'me' and 'mine'. There are followers and influence-peddlers, collectors of data, memories and feelings, reminders and prodders and monitors of causes and effects. We present ourselves to the world as a single being operating rationally from a single perspective and point of view, but inside, a whole society or regime is active.

Accustomed to looking at objects from an 'outside-standing' perspective, we may never have thought to look at the subject, to take into account the speaker's voice, the thinker's mind, the decision-maker's activities. We have been taught, or have assumed, that we are the ones who are feeling and thinking, determining meaning and making decisions. But when we look through the magnifying glass of awareness, we learn that mind is not just 'I, me, and mine'. We begin to see that mind is far more complex than we may have thought, and the process by which it translates perceptions into meaning is not necessarily a clear and orderly progression. While we have a sense of meaning that comes through thoughts and senses, feelings and thoughts themselves are not necessarily organized in a logical sequence, but combine and find expression in different ways.

We might imagine that just as the rhythms of speech shape sound into words, our decision-maker mind shapes meaning sequentially from awareness to consciousness to words and concepts. If our awareness were fully open, 360 degrees, we might be able to observe how this process operates. Until we can do this, however, we can say only that we experience reality through the filters of mind. We depend for meaning on mental processes that do not seem

Introduction

to connect in predictable ways. No wonder we are vulnerable to confusion and the problems that come in its wake.

For thousands of years, a question has plagued humanity: why does life have to have so many problems? Must we continue to experience frustration and confusion? Must we waste much of our lives in coping with emotional upheavals? Since it has always been this way, we may think we have no choice: "That is the way it is," we say. But can we question if this really has to be?

Problems are situations that we cannot resolve. They seem completely real, yet the circumstances we experience as a problem are conducted to us by mind. We can only think about the problem in the ways that mind allows, and mind operates through rules imprinted on its ways of perceiving and presenting reality, leaving us very few alternatives or solutions. If mind's way of operating blocks off all conceivable alternatives, there is nothing more we can do. We become fused to the problem as it has been set up by mind. For the most part, people just accept that this is the way things are. Yet, it seems important to give this matter serious thought and do what we can to resolve it. The

Introduction

need to initiate such a process inspired the idea of understanding presented here.

We are fortunate to be beneficiaries of knowledge gathered through many centuries of inquiry into every conceivable subject, but mind itself has seldom received the depth of attention necessary to ease its burdens and enable it to operate in happier and more creative ways. Mind has incredible power and flexibility, but uncared for and unguided it becomes a despot, limiting the ways we can know and respond, and subjecting us to confusion, anxiety and despair. If we wish to free ourselves of problems, we must become more aware of what mind is and what it needs.

We need an intelligent, creative, innovative way to study mind, one based on a gentle, detached observation that does not reinforce mind's tendency to grasp and concretize experience. This realization has inspired me to share my thoughts on mind with friends and associates within our Nyingma community. What began as informal exchanges developed into a more focused effort to express my way of thinking about a subject central to the quality of every human life.

In 2006, I met regularly with several senior students over a period of several months for talks and discussions intended to reveal where more

Introduction

detailed explanations were needed. In the course of these talks, I adopted the approach I felt would best illustrate important, but unfamiliar points which traditionally require a substantial context for understanding. Transcribed by Elizabeth Cook, these sessions were combined with earlier talks to provide a working manuscript. During the review process, this material was edited further and shaped into a more integrated presentation by Pema Gellek and Richard Dixey. After a third major review, the manuscript was brought to completion by Elizabeth Cook, Robin Caton, and Jack Petranker. All five editors are members of the faculty of Dharma College in Berkeley, California, where I had determined that this new form of understanding could be presented.

Although these talks were not intended to constitute a systematic presentation, the organization has taken on a certain order that reflects the unfolding quality of understanding itself. Since mind hears and expresses according to its own understanding, I have monitored the progress of this manuscript and intensively reviewed its contents with the editors several times. While I expected the editors to correct my dictated thoughts to standard English, some unusual uses of language have been deliberately retained.

Introduction

There is no stopping point, no end to the unfolding dynamic of understanding. As areas of misunderstanding are recognized and acknowledged, understanding manifests as necessary to resolve them. Each manifestation is a fresh revelation: While one may appear to contradict another, ultimately there are no contradictions, only different points of reference. All meanings are the unfolding of understanding, and all serve to dispel the negativity that shadows the human mind.

When understanding replaces misunderstanding, misunderstanding releases its hold and disappears, like the coils of a snake vanishing into its lair. With nothing left to act upon or correct, understanding quietly merges into the body of knowledge that informs our actions. Nothing remains that can be grasped; nothing remains that the self can appropriate and use for its benefit.

I realize that the approach I adopt here is unusual and that its perspectives may seem odd, even startling. Yet, from time to time I have been encouraged by glimpses of understanding in those who have given these thoughts serious consideration. These glimpses reveal that mind afflicted with problems can engage understanding in ways that dissolve these problems at their

Introduction

roots. Such understanding may be preliminary, with much more remaining to be understood. But it is my view that developed and fully extended, understanding can go far toward liberating the human mind.

May this volume benefit
all who seek understanding.

Sarvam Mangalam

Tarthang Tulku
Odiyan, Sonoma County, California
2013

How to Read this Book

Revelations of Mind is neither a traditional presentation of mind nor a philosophic or psychological system. My aim has been to introduce a universal approach to mind and mental processes rather than focusing on any specific viewpoint, system, or discipline. While Revelations touches on topics that readers may associate with philosophy, religion, psychology, or science, its orientation is more experiential and its style more impressionistic.

The whole of *Revelations of Mind* is an exercise for the mind, an unfolding of our mental experience intended to invite understanding that each person can access individually. Although practitioners of meditation may benefit in special ways, this book is addressed to any individual who appreciates the importance of developing a clearer understanding of his or her mind.

To activate this flow of understanding, you as the reader must be prepared to do your part. As you read, let go of the impulse to react too quickly to the points presented. Instead, just keep reading. Hear what is being said before you generate your own saying. If you can let your mind walk down this road without stumbling over a stone

How to Read This Book

here or a crack there, you will soon find that you can stride more broadly and exercise a more innovative way of reading.

If you would like to explore in more depth, I suggest you read this book several times. The first reading will let you become familiar with the concepts and gain an overall orientation to the major points presented. A second reading allows the mind to engage the topics on a more experiential level. I hope you will note a deeper sense of meaning as the words connect more directly to your own observation and intelligence. After this reading, you could perhaps say, "Now I recognize what is being pointed out."

The third reading moves deeper, toward seeing specific self-interpretations and readouts in action in your immediate experience. At this point, you could say, "Now I see what I am doing."

By the fourth reading, you may find yourself actually applying this way of understanding and gaining confidence through direct experience. Here you could say, "Now I understand what I am doing." Understanding can begin to reveal its own way of manifesting, its own way of commenting and pointing, and its own way of releasing.

How to Read This Book

When you have read the book four times, you may wish to make time for a two to four week retreat. This will give you a valuable opportunity to integrate this material and stabilize understanding on a sound foundation. Then you will be in a better position to take understanding to a higher level, where it becomes clear and inalienable.

To benefit most fully from what you read, contemplate it as if mind were hearing its own thoughts. Let mind read and feed back within itself, mind to mind, until clarity comes and mind understands. This is how mind naturally works, once we know how to give it the opportunity.

Since this book presents no system or doctrine, there is nothing to be gained from grasping at understanding when you sense it arising. At whatever level you are reading, mind is reading mind—generating mind interpretations and mind meanings, not final, fixed truths. Mind remains free to inquire into the source of each interpretation or to ask who is reading each level of meaning.

As you read, it is important to find your own individual way of looking, seeing, and tasting, your own way of viewing yourself and your journey. All the negative expressions of mind, from inflexibility and moodiness to self-centeredness

How to Read This Book

and ego solidity, are based on perception of your own fixed ways of juxtaposing. When you understand how this works and how it confines the mind and limits its natural brilliance, you can liberate yourself. When you act, your understanding will be different. One who knows the self and one who does not know the self will conduct themselves differently, because understanding and not understanding have different outcomes. The benefits and the virtuous power of the merit that action brings are different as well.

When you reach this stage, you will start to sense that you are gaining leverage of a new kind over your life, leverage that comes from knowledge. Whatever discipline you may practice, such as meditation or philosophy or education, you may have the increasing impression that creativity and protection are both coming your way. With a little understanding, mind has tools for working with the raw materials of mind's expression. It has a supportive friendship with itself, a shield against anxiety that allows new possibilities to emerge.

As you feel freer to engage your life experience in new ways, you may have a sense of something unfreezing deep within you. This indicates that your being is becoming more whole and your

1

The Central Importance of Mind

The study of mind is a vital and important subject, for mind is our life and the basis for our reality: its power is vast and its radiance illumines every aspect of our being. Active in every moment of our lives, mind governs our way of experiencing and influences how we respond to all that it presents. Wherever something is acting, creating, and energizing, wherever something is expanding or contracting, wherever there is suffering or pleasure, mind is revealing its presence. There is nothing in our experience that does not arise from mind, depend upon, and bear the imprint of mind.

Whether or not we are attuned to its activity, mind does the minding that sustains the momentum of our lives. Every instant, mind manifests through a complex array of operations, many on subliminal levels to which we have no access. Since it is difficult to question these inner operations of mind, our ways of understanding how mind gathers, presents, points out, and draws meaning out of the elements of our inner and outer environments are limited. Without knowing how mind processes and interprets this input, our ability to appreciate, cultivate, and direct the power of mind is constrained.

If we do not understand our minds, how can we have confidence in our motivations and decisions? What can we stand on as real? How can we know who we are? Lacking the knowledge even to begin to answer these questions, we have no choice but to suffer, for we do not know how or why our problems come about.

How Do We Understand Mind?

Over the past hundred years, much has been said about the conscious and unconscious mind, psychological archetypes, human behavior, the interaction of sense organs and brain, and the interaction of sensory data, mental concepts, and behavior. But even with the current interest in consciousness studies and the advances in neurology and imaging of the brain, our understanding of both brain and mind remains preliminary. Although theories abound, and science

I A Fresh Look at Mind

now has powerful tools for measuring aspects of mental activity and testing new insights, we are still working on the level of description, outlining the measurable operations of our neurological systems to gain a sense of what we could know from our own experience. But even this kind of knowledge remains one-dimensional and incomplete because it relies on perceptual and mental operations that themselves go unexamined.

Whether we start from a subjective or an objective orientation, we accept a dichotomy between self and everything else in the world it inhabits. This dichotomy comes up automatically in the process of cognition. Thus, we cannot avoid imposing the observer's viewpoint on even the most 'objective' phenomena. And the language we use to describe mind and interpret objective data is itself born of a dualistic perspective and the mental processes that reinforce it.

We say that mind discriminates and judges; we say that mind alone knows and that mind is responsible for identification, recognition, and decision-making. English has more than twenty different ways that the word 'mind' is used, and other languages may have yet other, different meanings. Each individual adds to this complicated brew a set of private meanings and connotations. The proliferation of meanings and definitions testifies to the archaic origins of words we apply to mind and raises doubts that we truly understand what we mean by 'mind'. We might wonder what deeper meanings have been lost through millennia of transmission, or ask what outmoded associations might be inhibiting a fresh perspective. If we could give mind a different name, might we open a new frontier for understanding?

A New Way of Exploring

Normally we rely on the conceptual apparatus that mind makes available. Now the time has come to enter the inner realm of mind and understand how it operates on all levels of our being. But where might we find a point of entry to this realm? We would like to question mind directly, but mind seems reluctant to show itself. For all our methods of rational inquiry, for all our treasury of concepts and philosophical systems, it seems that we do not yet have the tools we need to explore the mysterious territory of our own minds.

When we consider the difficulties of understanding exactly what mind is and what it does,

I A Fresh Look at Mind

when we attempt to look more closely at the structures that condition our knowledge of self and world, we begin to appreciate how little we really know. Despite pretenses to the contrary, at some level we sense the power of mind to override our intentions, dismiss our questions, and determine the outcome of every moment of experience. Usually unacknowledged or brushed aside as we deal with the more immediate pressures of life, this sense that we must endure whatever mind presents is an ongoing source of insecurity and fear.

However reluctant we may be to engage this topic, our own readiness to dismiss, deny, or reason our discomfort away should give us pause: Why do we shy away from exploring the insecurity that lies at the root of our being? Doesn't our fear tell us that at a deeper level we know that such fundamental ignorance is not acceptable?

The knowledge that this kind of disquiet affects every human on this planet can motivate us to re-examine what we do know of mind on the basis of our own experience. Perhaps we cannot look at the face of mind directly, but we can examine its processes more closely, asking how they were set up and how it is that within the infinite possibilities for human experience, we

The Central Importance of Mind

have so little choice in what we think and feel. In questioning the operations of mind, we might discover how to guide them in ways that ensure a better outcome for our lives.

This inquiry challenges us to strip away the veils of assumptions and denial so that we can see how our efforts to be free are undermined—not by others (as we so often think)—but by the orientation and operations of our own minds. The more honestly we can acknowledge the extent of our not-knowing, the more mind will open, allowing the light of understanding to illuminate what is not yet known. In the process, we may experience a most inspiring insight: there is more to be understood, and more to be revealed, by a mind fully engaged in understanding.

2

Mind and 'I'

If mind is central to all aspects of our lives, it is in our best interest to develop a satisfying rapport with mind and make it a good friend. With a clearer understanding of the nature of mind, how it operates, and how it communicates to our conscious awareness, we could be more consistently at ease with our thoughts and feelings, more comfortable in our embodiment, and more confident in exercising our capacities for creativity and meaningful accomplishment. Viewing our mind as a partner we might find it possible to direct its power into a mutually supportive relationship with our own being, a kind and nurturing relationship, a profound, perhaps even enlightening relationship.

Considering how language presents 'I' and mind as discrete entities and fosters distinctions between them, the notion of a partnership that called this separation into doubt would seem promising. But it does not appear that this potentially useful line of inquiry has been widely pursued.

Perspectives on Mind and 'I'

We generally use the word 'I' to point to ourselves. Here we use 'I' in this same familiar, non-technical way to explore how concepts of mind and 'I' operate in the context of everyday experience.

In everyday dialogue, 'I' seems close and intimate, the voice of personal identity, an active agent that some disciplines refer to as ego or self. In contrast, 'mind' seems more general, perhaps more all-encompassing and remote, more difficult to point to and describe.

But this is just a first approximation. The relationship between mind and 'I' is not fully clear. Sometimes mind is viewed as the thought-producing aspect of our being, the provider of ideas, comments, and interpretations that 'I' can then express. In this context, mind may be sensed as a presence that can criticize, demand, or warm the heart with good feelings. It can also be an annoyance, nagging about trivia when we wish to concentrate, sleep, or just be quiet. In darker moments, mind can become a source of pain, flooding the cells of body and brain with

I A Fresh Look at Mind

mind does not always accept what 'I' want to do. It speaks through 'my' nerves and muscles; it aches, complains, and holds back. We may sense it murmuring silently in the background of experience, making comments that surface as 'my' own thoughts: "I am not happy. I am bored. I am tired. I really do not want to do this." As soon as these thoughts are voiced, they become 'mine'. 'I' take possession of the feelings flickering within body and mind. Mind signals, "I am bored," and without knowing quite why, 'I' find myself becoming restless and sleepy.

Usually, we would not think to question what is so clearly the case. Yes, I am bored, and so of course I feel restless and sleepy. Yet if we do pose the question, matters may take a different turn. If we ask, "Who is saying this? Who is bored?" the sense of boredom may lift. Such questions put the mind in an unusual posture. Mind seems reluctant to assert itself when challenged to take on the role of 'I' directly.

3

The Business of Mind

'I' by its nature tends to assume ownership of all aspects of our being. I, myself, my reality, my mind, my body, my feelings—all are mine, all belong to me. But in the very moment 'I' is firmly enthroned, mind comes forth to take an even more authoritative role. 'I' may be the owner, but mind expresses, points out, and establishes order. Dividing everything it perceives into right/wrong, useful/useless, good/bad, mind lays down laws like a king giving orders: "This is the right way to be and to act."

The Regime of Mind

As the king of our being, mind projects its power through operations that administer and coordinate all of our mental and physical functions. Operating as awareness, consciousness, perception, or through other processes called by other

I A Fresh Look at Mind

names, mind collects and distills input from our senses; it cognizes, identifies, and re-cognizes. It confirms and re-confirms what has been identified and recognized. It labels and spells out the meaning of everything we find conceivable. It points out and interprets meaning, then announces it properly in language we can understand. Together, these operations of mind set up a powerful regime that controls the nature of our experience from moment to moment.

Throughout each day of our lives, the regime of mind continues to monitor, identify, interpret, and report on every feature of experience, substantial and insubstantial, concrete and abstract, internal and external. Mind processes all these diverse streams of input into a steady flow of meanings and associations, producing the thoughts and feelings that enrich our experience and bring it alive.

Mind also integrates and interprets input from 'I' and the senses, reporting on what experience means from the perspective of 'me': "This is pleasing, this makes 'me' happy." "This is not good, this is painful, this makes 'me' miserable." The business of mind is multiple: it coordinates impulses and signals from the body and senses,

The Business of Mind

it carries out its own internal 'minding' operations, and it empowers 'I', 'me' and 'mine' by interpreting experience in ways that affirm their various identities as subject, object, and owner.

As mind labels, points out meaning, monitors, and interprets, the constant flow of its 'minding' provides a seemingly solid matrix for our experience to take place. Rarely stilled, this 'minding' generates a sense of continuity that shapes the way our experience unfolds and reassures us of the reality of all we perceive.

4

Mind and Language

If mind is the king of our being, language, its medium of expression, is surely its prime minister. Language gives mind a voice that communicates externally, with other people. But language also communicates within, mind to mind, mind to heart, and mind to psyche or soul. Through language, mind makes itself known to our conscious awareness and, through language we express mind's interpretations of our experience and observations. Language and mind are natural allies, intimately involved in operating our physical and mental processes.

Because of the way mind generates and applies language, we tend to accept as real all that mind identifies and pronounces, as well as all that mind presents to us as memories and recollections. Usually this acceptance occurs subliminally, below the level of our conscious awareness. Only when we look more closely at mind's relationship to language can we appreciate how strongly this interaction impacts our lives.

Mind and Language

Sound, Shape and Meaning

From experience, we know that mind is acutely sensitive to sound, and that it responds to the subtle nuances that carry meaning directly from ear to brain. An image alone may not be sufficient: Mind requires a second kind of marker to confirm an object's identity and distinguish it from all other possibilities. This is what sound provides.

Of all identifiers available to the human mind, sound registers most strongly and offers the broadest range of features. Mind combines the elements of sound—pitch, intensity, duration, and rhythm—into phrases capable of transmitting complex, highly differentiated meanings. These elements are the basic components of language; they give words the power to resonate like music at the core of our being.

It is interesting to contemplate how perfectly eye, mind, and ear work together to shape sound into language, a vehicle of profound power and significance. When we pay close attention to the words that emerge through thought or speech, we can note that each word represents an internal marriage of sound and image. The sound comes, and the image is immediately available, because the mind has learned the shape that this sound

I   A Fresh Look at Mind

represents: in merging sound with shape, mind has captured the meaning. Now sound, shape, and meaning are imprinted in mind, fused into a convenient label that can be pronounced and recalled in three-dimensional detail whenever the impulse arises.

Strengthened by usage into words and concepts, labels merge into the structure of our language and gain certainty through repetition. They become the content of 'our' thoughts, thoughts that engage and re-engage our perceptual processes while accumulating additional nuances of meaning. Networks of associations develop that can then be activated instantly by the sound of a label. Mind continues to affirm their reality throughout our lives.

Guarantor of Accuracy

Once mind has a label prepared that applies to specific sensory impulses, that label carries significance that cannot be dismissed. When mind meets a similar perception again, it identifies it instantly through a process of exclusion: this is a chair, because mind has identified a similar object as a chair before. Mind knows the essential character of that label, and no other label in

Mind and Language

its collection fits so precisely. Mind recognizes the object, stamps it with meanings previously assigned, and projects it back to the mind, where it is confirmed and enriched through associations with past perceptions and experiences.

This process—sensory vibrations, identity, labeling, recognition, confirmation, interpretations, and associations—sustains a kind of automatic feedback system that plays out and rewinds within the mind like an endlessly repeating tape. In this way, mind bears witness to itself, confirming and re-confirming that the object has been accurately pointed out and the meaning correctly conveyed. If there are other interpretations and meanings, they belong to another category or situation and apply to different purposes. Mind has already excluded them. In effect, mind is reassuring itself, even as it reassures us: "This is the right interpretation, guaranteed to be accurate."

Through this process of exclusion, mind designs the frame of our reality. It determines all we can perceive, think about, and know. In determining the precise positioning of words and concepts, it shapes the rules that govern how objects are to be named and identified, the fundamental principles of exclusion and polarity, and the

I A Fresh Look at Mind

grammatical rules that enable us to understand, interpret, and communicate meaning to others.

Language, Custom-Made

While based on standards shared by society and culture, language is also custom-tailored to fit each individual who uses it. Much as a contractor works from a blueprint to build a house, mind adopts the basic framework and patterns of language transmitted to it early in life, then integrates its store of names and concepts and associated objects and meanings into the structure already established. The 'house' built by mind suits us perfectly, because mind has adapted it according to our individual preferences, experience, and needs. It is truly custom-made.

It is as if mind has established a business whose principal product is language, with the 'I' as its primary customer. Language conveys meaning not only to others but also to our own conscious awareness. Having pointed out and identified sensory impressions, mind uses language to label perceptions, to interpret and confirm them in light of previous experience, and to transmit them to us in ways that establish a sense of reality or truth. This mass of data feeds

Mind and Language

back to the mind, yielding meaning that can now be expressed. As mind agrees with the feedback it has received, we gain confidence in the reality of what we now 'know'. We buy the product that mind has produced.

Once this process is set in place, the whole system operates smoothly. Mind has its sources and suppliers—our senses and awareness. It knows how to run its operations, how to please its customer, and how to enforce the rules of the system so they cannot be broken.

It seems there is no ground for complaint. Mind serves its customer well, providing the words and meanings 'I' use to orient myself and identify everything in 'my' surroundings, as well as the content for thoughts, memories, and imaginings. 'I' accept without question what mind makes available, confident that it will serve the purpose. This process continues automatically throughout the course of our lives. The notion of an alternative simply does not arise.

Because these products of mind accumulate, we tend to feel that our knowledge is increasing. Yet can we, as mind's customers, trust that these products are sufficient to advance our knowledge and deepen our understanding? Depending on

I   A Fresh Look at Mind

mind for structure and meaning, we may never have looked closely at how mind established the basis for this structure, how it makes and enforces the rules for its operation, how it interprets words and concepts and applies their meanings. In satisfying our needs, does mind exclude potentially productive lines of inquiry? Does its structure limit the products available to us, like the factories in a totalitarian state?

Since the language of interpretation is established within the mind, it can be examined further. At any given point in the realm of mind, we can survey what we know and investigate what we would like to find out. Of course, everything that operates within this realm is part of the mind-business under investigation. This means that what we are investigating is ordinary knowledge—knowledge that relies on language custom-made for us and reinforced by every movement of our mind. For this level of understanding, our custom-made language serves us well. But it is not certain that mind can use it to recognize experience for which no label has been established.

5

Rules for Reality

Mind's way of processing language reveals that it is capable of establishing strong dichotomies. We see this tendency in the cycles of recognition and confirmation that reverberate through mind over and over, like instant replays of contested plays in sports. This ability to divide itself into two distinct, often contradictory roles underlies the logic of the rules mind has established for assigning names and labels.

Activating reflexively in every instant of perception, this dichotomy serves to establish and maintain the dualistic perspective that separates self as subject from everything else in the objective, 'knowable' world. It comes up the moment an object presents itself for identification. Mind grasps, and instantly the sound of the label arises. Recognition that there is something 'out there' calls attention to what is 'in here'. This response activates mind's logical sense of positioning and gives rise to the roles of subject and

I A Fresh Look at Mind

object. With this, the concept of 'I' comes into play: I, as subject, am aware of the object (an image, form, transition, or action). On the most fundamental level, language enshrines this dualistic way of perception as its operating system and imposes it on all of mind's expressions. We accept and follow the rules because this kind of body/mind interaction is familiar and has meaning for us.

As mind points out sensory impressions and characteristics, it distinguishes shapes, colors, right-ness or wrong-ness, likes and dislikes, and pain or pleasure, and associates them with labels previously assigned. According to rules it has received or created independently, it makes judgments: this is right, this is wrong; like this, don't like that; this is real, this is true; that may not be real or true. While there are various shades in between, mind's interpretations follow the same basic pattern: agreeable/not agreeable, acceptable/not acceptable, and so on. These pronouncements imprint strongly on consciousness, where they shape our attitudes and ways of thinking.

Since the features of mental activity are closely interconnected, with no gaps in between, perceptions are immediately sealed and accepted as 'how things are'. Once this process begins, it establishes the framework for our view of reality. Accepting this mind-created framework as real, we can only act within it.

Having established patterns that sustain its sense of rightness and order, mind continues to monitor perceptions and thoughts. Now subtly, now more firmly, mind shepherds us continuously: "This is the correct way; this way is not." "Yes." "No." "Maybe." Mind has already scoped out the territory and claimed it—now it is exercising its power to direct everything we think and do. Constantly vigilant, mind creates, monitors, and maintains the inner environment of our lives through inner dialogues that continue day and night.

Setup for Agitation

Mind's reliance on dichotomy tends to invite indecision, misunderstandings and confusion that agitate mind and cause us needless suffering. Conflict creates blockages that invite 'second thoughts'—opinions, doubts, and uncertainties that activate both sides of the dichotomy simultaneously. The need to maintain the positions of both sides causes perceptions, thoughts, and

I A Fresh Look at Mind

what is happening and everything associated with it as real. This sense of certitude merges with our sense of self and the meanings mind produces. Mind knows for sure that an object has been accurately identified, and the ongoing momentum of its minding process removes any residues of doubt. With no independent way to discriminate reality from illusion, whether mind operates in a way that leads to resolution and clarity, or embroils us in confusion and conflicts, we have to engage our surroundings in the way mind interprets and presents them to us. Such is the power of mind, power that we draw upon continually in making sense of our experience.

This Is the Way It Is

We speak of consciousness, conscience, desires, regret, anger, love, and more, and identify a wide range of emotional and psychological patterns. But these are all specific manifestations of mind—products that we give different names, buy into, consume, and incorporate into our way of being.

Everyone manifests emotional and psychological patterns, but which ones surface most strongly or readily seems to depend on environ-

Rules for Reality

ment, circumstances, and genetic or other factors. One individual may tend to experience anxiety more often than anger; another may be more inclined to avoid than to confront, to become hesitant or insecure rather than overconfident.

At some point, individuals identify themselves with particular products of mind, in much the same way that people are drawn to certain brands of products that support their self-image. They may shape their fantasies and desires accordingly, or identify with certain kinds of music, or take up concepts or forms of language that enhance characteristics they admire. Doing this can provide a sense of personal empowerment. Accepting the products of minds as their own, they become strongly convinced of the reality of whatever it is they identify with. "This is the way it is, this is the way I am, this is the way I should be."

6

Customer Mind

Mind relates to the whole of our being, and its qualities manifest in all we think, feel, and do. Since mind pervades every aspect of our reality, we might say that mind is our entire reality. But for most of us it seems more natural to think of reality as being 'out there', somehow apart from our selves, consisting of objects and events we can define and categorize.

We tend to objectify and define mind in the same way. For instance, we may state with some certainty that the brain is a physical organ that relates to the body's nerves and senses, while mind is more associated with the psyche, which is less localized and more diffuse. But what is the basis of this certainty? A closer look might reveal that the process of definition is in fact ongoing and open-ended, suggesting that our understanding of these concepts is far from conclusive. Instead, we unthinkingly apply labels and categories, confidently pointing out what purpose each

Customer Mind

one serves. Analyzing the aspects of mind intellectually, much as we would point out the names and functions of the components of a computer, we distance our sense of 'I' from mind.

Without inquiring how the mind-system was set up, 'I' am content to take charge of its operation. The truth is that we cannot separate ourselves from mind and observe it directly, so we cannot verify what mind really is. Yet, convinced by a false sense of resolution, 'I' can assume charge of mind's operations because mind has become familiar, an object that 'I' can name and relate to as real.

Comfortable with our conclusions, we may see no reason to investigate further. Like an architect drafting the plans of a building, we move on to compartmentalize and define all aspects of experience, including the functions of mind. Everything has a label, and every label has a story, complete with its purpose and meaning. The meanings assigned to the labels take care of all the specifics.

Creator and Customer

Thinking we know, we rely for meaning on our concepts and the stories that accumulate around

I A Fresh Look at Mind

them. We act on this basis, and our actions have consequences through the operation of cause and effect. By the very way it operates, mind maintains the conditions for cause and effect and develops the patterns that perpetuate disappointment and pain. But, unless we understand how mind produced these patterns through identifying, labeling, and recognition, our concepts and stories have no real basis. This means that we lack access to the full significance of our actions. We do not fully understand why we do what we do, we cannot foresee the effects of our actions, and we do not realize what patterns we are establishing for our lives. We can only learn by trial and error, a method guaranteed to be wasteful and potentially destructive.

To examine more deeply, we need to know what lies behind this system: who set it up? Who is receiving this information, who is the user, and who is monitoring and updating it? There does not seem to be much clarity on these issues. Instead, patterns of thought become so habitual that we rarely notice them in operation.

Mind participates in this process as both creator and 'customer'. It creates the timing and continuity that enable cause and effect to take place; it initiates actions and renders them automatic through the processes of identity and recognition. As 'customer', mind also receives the product—consequences that are welcome or unwelcome, depending on the clarity that informed the actions. Participating in both cause and effect, mind perpetuates patterns that leave us vulnerable to confusion, frustration and pain, and it enforces these patterns by convincing us that they are real and 'right'.

Is There Nothing Other Than Mind?

This question is worth careful consideration. Only mind knows how to spell out the features, the names, and the qualities of everything we can perceive. Mind is the anchor of the news show put on by our inner broadcasting system, the one who collects data from our organs and senses, compiles and interprets it, then broadcasts it, laying out our reality in forms we can act upon.

Like a chef, mind presents the menu and the schedule for preparing and producing it. Mind selects and combines the ingredients it deems necessary, then places before us the completed meal. All we need to do is accept it and take it in. Whether we enjoy the meal or suffer indigestion

I A Fresh Look at Mind

afterwards depends upon the quality and wholesomeness of the ingredients mind has provided.

Similarly, for everything we do, mind sets up the framework and we fill in the details. We expect mind to do its job, and we are expected to do ours. Normally, we do not think to question how mind does its job. But now we are ready to take a more active role, to learn how mind designed the systems that have such significance to our lives. Only then can we determine how these systems might be modified or if entirely different systems might work better for us today.

If we look inward and contemplate how experience takes shape and form, at some point we may realize that reality is established by mind-telling and mind-dialoguing, mind-feeling, and mind-interpreting, all on the basis of a dualistic perspective that sets us up for problems. Perhaps mind developed this system in ages past to communicate meaning to consciousness. But since we are the ones who have accepted it, we may have the option to consider an alternative.

As unique individuals who have each matured within a certain array of physical, social, emotional, psychic, and environmental conditions, each of us must investigate for ourselves the specific system that governs our reality and determine how best to improve it. But below the specifics of individual identity flows a deeper, more universal current that connects us to the qualities we associate with human being. Reflecting on the beauty that mind is capable of transmitting, we may recall moments when love, joy, and gratitude have broken through the fog of our mind-created stories and illuminated every cell of our bodies. Surely we can transform the regime that now blocks our voluntary access to this power. Surely mind can become more generous with its riches and end the games that set us up for disappointment and despair!

This is our very own journey, a journey that leads to the heart of our being. It begins with making friends with our mind and observing what it reveals in the context of our own experience.

7

Mind on Automatic

Mind accommodates feedback from the senses as well as from its own operations. As it does so, it automatically imposes its processes on whatever input it receives. Mind moves instantly to respond to questions, situations, and challenges and to deal with all variations of experience, while also coping with the pushback from its own patterns. Since its nature is to respond, it cannot avoid engaging whatever presents itself, even when engaging them activates patterns of denial or drives them deep into our subconscious, where they foster resentment, fear, and negativity.

This process is dynamic and inclusive. Impressions flow in from all directions, stimulating interpretations and mingling with commentaries and emotions already in progress. So much can be happening at once—seeing, hearing, tasting, touch, scent, thoughts, images, happiness, pain, terror, guilt trips, anxiety, passion, and aggression. With all these streams of data competing for attention, mind is fully occupied from moment to moment.

Cycles of Feedback and Response

Self-imposing and self-projecting, mind allows all manner of expressions to manifest, then repossesses and recycles them back into its systems, where they become the bases for new cycles of projections, interpretations, judgments, and feedback. It is mind that says 'yes' or 'no', or hesitates in between, perhaps listening to its own echoes. From time to time, it may get caught up in negotiating with itself, as if questioning its own interpretations. "It could be this, or it could be that. If it is this, that could happen, and I don't think I want that. But if it is that, this will happen. That might be all right. But what if it isn't?"

The mental traffic that results from all this activity can jam the flow of thoughts and images, so that very little else can get through. Even when the traffic runs more smoothly, it still occupies the mind continuously, clouding the open clarity of our mental environment and setting the stage for distraction. Yet this is mind as we know it, and we have to live with it.

I A Fresh Look at Mind

As mind takes in whatever is presented, interpretations come up instantly, almost magically, with great sharpness and immediacy. As questioner, mind asks, "Is this ok?" As responder, mind verifies, "Yes, that is right," giving its seal of approval. Having no way to join in this dialogue, we can only accept what mind decides.

Mind's regime of associations, interpretations, and commentary takes over automatically and immediately. If we look closely, especially when mind is quiet, we can sense mind's retinue approaching: a few thoughts, then feelings, perhaps a sudden surge of anger as memory recalls how someone took advantage of us a few days before, or a brighter outlook as ideas or urges take our thoughts toward daydreams and the anticipation of pleasure. Within an instant, we are completely immersed, already responding to whatever scenario the regime has imposed. There is little we can do to distract it—mind will keep going, identifying and commenting according to its own rhythms, according to what it has learned to interpret as 'right'.

While this kind of automation speeds processing and offers convenience, when it takes over our consciousness in this way, we might

Mind on Automatic

well question the cost. What price might we be paying for this ever-expanding accumulation of patterns and the proliferation of an ever more efficient automation?

Accustomed to the rhythms of thoughts and dialogues that direct an inner chain of reactions, we tend to notice very little of what is going on around us in real time. What we experience are the thoughts and feelings prompted by the recycling and interpretation that follow upon identity and recognition. We react, but the primary perception is long past: we are experiencing echoes of the original, presented in our custom-made language, as interpreted and revised by mind's regime. While we may be fully connected to the elements at work in the regime, we are out of touch with the actual experience that gave rise to the regime's activity. This disconnection leaves us vulnerable to forgetfulness, mistakes, and misinterpretations, all of which feed uncertainty and confusion back into the mechanisms of mind.

Throughout our lives, we live within this mind-created realm, cut off from the immediacy of experience and subject to the dictates and interpretations of mind's regime. Within this realm, the regime holds sway. Everything mind

I   A Fresh Look at Mind

presents—even the most toxic feelings and emotions, even extreme anxiety and physical pain—is acceptable, because on a very fundamental level we have empowered mind to feed back to us the regime's interpretations and meanings.

Does Mind Know What It Is Doing?

Mind recognizes and interprets continuously, but it appears that we are missing out on much of its activity, for at any point during our day we can remember very little of what we were thinking during our prior waking hours. Perhaps this lapse in recall indicates that we are not always consciously directing our minds in purposeful activity. At best we might say that our periods of purposeful activity are continually interrupted by less focused mental operations.

If we suppose that this is true not just for us, but for every human being, then it is fair to say that the minds of seven billion people are churning more or less without direction for at least five or six hours every day, and probably much more, generating thoughts, making decisions, and motivating actions. This would amount to a total of roughly forty billion mind-hours lost in generating idle thoughts, planning for the future,

Mind on Automatic

indulging fantasies, chewing on resentments, coping with desires, fretting over worries, awash in emotionality, obsessing over concerns, frozen in fear, or spiraling into depression and despair. This amounts to some 60,000 entire human lifetimes each day that are not engaged in productive activity. Assuming that thoughts tend to manifest in ways that influence others, such erratic mental activity must have far-reaching effects.

Seen in this light, a simple question takes on much greater weight: Does mind really know what it is doing? Mind monitors our internal processes; it calculates, plans, and initiates with some efficiency. But it does not seem so intent on revealing the source of our difficulties or removing obstacles that prevent us from transcending them.

I A Fresh Look at Mind

sort or another, each of which will add new layers of complexity. The instant mind identifies a problem, recognition triggers the whole mechanism of response. If we have no way to 'un-recognize' the problem, the responses it arouses can hit us in the head and the heart, arousing our feelings with great force and throwing our whole being into turmoil. Mind becomes blocked, with no clear path to resolution.

At this point, attempts to deny the problem may only increase the pressure; on the other hand, acknowledging the problem tends to validate it and perpetuate its effects. Holding on to the position of 'having a problem', we have to endure the mind-created anxieties and emotions that go with it, for mind is now operating in its 'problem' mode. The more we try to suppress these reactions, the more we re-cognize and re-validate them, and the more persistently they return.

Later, when mind calms down, we may wonder what all the upset was about. But this insight is momentary. The pattern is likely to repeat, and residues of confusion and unresolved emotions accumulate with each repetition. This kind of inner struggle opens the door to self-doubt, insecurity, and anxieties that lurk in the background

Identifier Mind

of mind like enemies awaiting their opportunity to attack.

While most of us prefer to think that we are calm, balanced, rational, and 'can hold it together', even the most intelligent mind is vulnerable to this kind of agitation. Ignoring this vulnerability, or erecting walls around it, will not prevent agitation from arising. At some point, most likely when we are least able to deal with it, a situation will penetrate whatever defenses we have erected, and we may be unable to respond effectively.

Even in good times, much of our life is lost to the ups and downs of mind's distractions and its black holes of worry and depression. Knowing this, we know as well that we have a precious opportunity to understand the foundations of our doubts and fears and free ourselves from needless suffering. Can we try now, before we meet with problems so overwhelming that they could seriously impact the course of our lives?

Mind Itself has the Solution

There seems to be a certain shyness in the West about connecting problems too closely to the workings of the mind. The general tendency is to assume that most problems come from an exter-

I A Fresh Look at Mind

nal source. "I don't have any money." "I don't have the knowledge I need." Even sophisticated and accomplished persons tend to trace problems to events beyond their control. It is as if everyone has been somehow manipulated into looking in only one direction and thinking in only one way, applying a knowledge mass-produced and sold to each individual mind as the sole standard for functioning well and exercising control.

Even when we see the value of changing this situation, it can be very difficult to relax our hold on what we believe—or want to believe—is right and real. This can be especially true if we think that doing so might affect how others judge us. People who care very much how others feel about them tend to cultivate and present a particular image, even if that image is a negative one. Unexamined, even a negative self-image can become the anchor for an individual's personality and sense of empowerment to the extent that losing it would leave him or her with no sense of place or position. Even when struggling in the worst of circumstances, such persons may go to great lengths to uphold their image, thinking, "I cannot lose my position, I cannot lose my dignity!" Anything—even physical or psychological pain—might be endured more easily than humiliation.

Identifier Mind

Preoccupation with this kind of 'dignity' isolates us from our own experience. It makes us strangers to ourselves, reluctant to look too closely at what lies inside. When we cling tightly to this perspective, it becomes nearly impossible to look meaningfully at the workings of mind. Ignored, allowed to continue without intervention or guidance, the mechanisms of mind will become more rigid and oppressive over time. As patterns intensify and residues accumulate, mind will present us with problems that are ever more crippling and painful.

9

The Victimizing Mind

Nearly everyone assigns great importance to business, career, and family, and builds his or her life around these central features of our society. Some are successful, others have to struggle to find their way; some experience strong ups and downs, and some fail to get anywhere on their own. Everyone is vulnerable: Life is unpredictable and offers few guarantees.

Successful or not, some people may end up lonely and hopeless, their truest thoughts and feelings sealed deep inside. Finding it difficult to inspire themselves or take encouragement from positive advice, they may have no one they trust to counsel them. Eventually they may see nothing of much value, not even in themselves. Their self-esteem weakens; they withdraw more and more. As their inner environment darkens and takes on a quality of mourning, the senses draw in, and pressure builds internally. Thoughts and

The Victimizing Mind

memories turn negative and become sources of pain. They cannot trust and they cannot reach out for help. Finally, there is nothing they can do.

All of us have some experience with these ways of being. When we hear expressions of self-doubt and discouragement—"I am unhappy," "I'm not doing the right thing." "This doesn't seem worth it." "This is not what I wanted to do, but I have no choice"—we understand what they mean. We may not use the same words, but we can relate to the feelings behind them because we have felt something similar.

How can we respond? There are powerful medicines for physical illnesses, but our ability to reverse such a drift into hopelessness and depression remains limited. Some use drugs to ease their pain and turn their minds in a more positive direction, but these may provide only temporary relief or have unforeseen outcomes. Surely we would like more lasting and reliable solutions that benefit the whole of our being.

Mind's Sensitivity

The root cause for this kind of suffering is a lack of understanding what mind is and what it needs to fill us with the joy and beauty that can be

1 A Fresh Look at Mind

realized in even the most humble surroundings. Even people who have invested time and energy in exploring various routes to inner knowledge may have given little thought to how our minds process input from our senses and feelings. Yet this kind of understanding seems crucial. Sensitive to our feelings, our minds pick up resentful, distrustful, even paranoid images and project them back into the ongoing streams of perception. They build up and intensify negative input, providing labels that appear to fit our frustration and emotions. We discriminate in all the ways the mind has learned—unfair, unjust, right or wrong, real or unreal—and we act them out. The words associated with these reactions are spoken through the mouth and taken in through the ears; mind hears and responds, setting in motion new cycles of cause and effect. Words have consequences: once spoken, they imprint meanings and images on the mind that are difficult, possibly impossible to erase. Their effects can ripple through consciousness for a long time.

The Game-Playing Mind

Yesterday we may have felt as though we were in the hell realms; today, perhaps we are in a happier place. Tomorrow, we may be somewhere

The Victimizing Mind

else. Mind makes available all the realms accessible through human experience, from the frozen and burning hells to celestial realms of continuous delight.

Reflecting on this, we might find it difficult to believe that we have the power to choose what realm we wish to experience. But since experience comes through the mind, the flavor and quality of our experience largely depends on the way we use our minds. Identity, labeling, validation, and interpretation form the mind-regime that structures experience, and this regime is the reason we have problems. How we view this regime and relate to it has important implications for all aspects of life.

Up to now, we could always blame our problems on others, on the way things are, or on causes and conditions outside our control. Now we may see that we have a choice: We can continue to play this game with our minds for the rest of our lives, assuring that we will remain insecure, vulnerable to problems that can pop up at any moment. Or we can make a better choice: understanding.

To determine the value of understanding, we have only to observe what happens when we do

I A Fresh Look at Mind

not understand how our minds produce and process our thoughts and attitudes. We all regularly plant and cultivate fantasies, posturing, excuses, and denials. However harmless they may seem at the time, the games we play in this way plant thoughts and images in the mind. When this kind of planting, cultivation, and re-seeding is repeated over many years, it can be difficult to separate ourselves from the convoluted images and attitudes that these games perpetuate.

When we see someone in distress and disoriented, unable to play the usual games in the usual way, when we see such a person falling victim to whatever thoughts and imaginings his or her mind projects, we witness first-hand the helpless vulnerability, the nightmarish fantasies, and the anger and hostility they have to endure as mind wanders in confusion, drifting from happier realms to the hells. Once mind has gone to those dark places, it can be very difficult to pull it back.

When we get into difficulty, we tend to rely on experts. But experts are human beings too; their knowledge is limited and they have similar human problems. Ultimately, for some situations, there is no solution. We are in the realm of the conditioned, dualistic mind, responding to what-

The Victimizing Mind

ever arises from moment to moment and vulnerable to misunderstanding, conflicted feelings, and emotional pain. Not knowing where our choices are leading—or if we even have choices—we participate in cycles of cause and effect and become caught up in them. Even if we have not intentionally caused a situation, when the results begin to manifest we can only endure whatever happens.

When we observe the suffering that mind can inflict, when we realize we are ultimately helpless to control our own responses or to ease the pain of loved ones lost in confusion, we understand that this is not a happy situation. Seeing this, we have the knowledge we need to question, "Does it have to be this way?"

Victims of Mind's Regime

If we ask why we feel anxious or have low self-esteem, now we may understand, "Mind is telling us this, and we have accepted it. We have obeyed its rules, and it is confirming that this response is the proper one." For example, suppose mind says, "You are a failure. Others were depending on you, and you let them down. How can anyone trust you again?" What choice do we have but to go along? Consciously or subconsciously, we

10

Dependence on Identity

Identity is key to the reality-creating program that mind operates. We believe in identity—our own and that of everything around us. It is as if mind has provided us with a card bearing our image and the label, 'I am'. More fundamental than credit cards or the usual legal proofs that identify our names, addresses, and vital information, mind's identity card serves as our own special label: it validates our existence and confirms our sense of ourselves as unique individuals. It represents the qualities we wish to project to the outside world; it reveals the views we hold of ourselves and fits in seamlessly with mind's way of establishing reality.

Processing sensory data, identifying what is and excluding what is not, assessing right and wrong, judging what is desirable and what is undesirable, mind is constantly scanning and verifying the labels that convey the full meaning

Dependence on Identity

of its products. This is how mind sustains the identity of 'I' and supplies the sense of security we have come to depend upon in viewing ourselves as independent beings. Identity gives us a sense of status and focus that our customer-mind views as essential. It is useful, it helps us fit in with others, and it generally appears to be working well.

Because our identity depends upon it, carrying mind's identity card requires our full focused attention twenty-four hours a day, seven days a week. Coded into it are all the labels and associations that apply to every aspect of experience, as well to as our jobs, status, associations, education, and the qualities we wish to project. With our card, we can present ourselves to others in ways that they can recognize and respect: we have the right qualifications, we can be counted on to behave in acceptable ways, and we are responsible. Now we can conduct business; we have the power and position we need.

Of course, we need to be loyal to the identity the card confirms, and we need to fulfill the functions and obligations this symbol represents, regardless of how our feelings, aspirations, and situation may change over time.

I A Fresh Look at Mind

Of all the functions of mind, the ability to establish our identity—the 'me', the 'I', the self—may be the most important, because without it we have nothing. What if we reached for our card and it were not there? Even the thought that it might be lost is threatening. Once we have it, however secure we may feel in our sense of 'me', 'I', and self, we need to protect, use, and be fully responsible for it. We need to validate it over and over again.

Why Is Understanding Identity Important?

Everything essential to experience as we know it, including consciousness, thought, and senses, is conveyed through the operation of identity. Invisible, it affects the course of every interaction. Interpretations take shape within its realm of influence. Mind points out and identity designates accordingly: this is right, that is wrong; accommodate this, reject that. All this is done from the perspective of an 'I', 'me' or 'self', in accordance with the rules for subject/object polarity that mind itself has established.

But what is behind this operation? This is difficult to determine, because we cannot see into that space. Since identity happens and objects

Dependence on Identity

appear, we assume that these objects occupy some kind of space, but we cannot tell what occupied that same space before the objects appeared or after they are gone. We cannot know if there is an unoccupied openness behind the operation of identity that allows for origination to come about independently.

What we generally call 'mind' encompasses senses, perception, and all kinds of thoughts that arise and move in and out, shifting our view back and forth between subjective and objective orientations. All the while, identity is functioning, sustaining a continuous flow of recognition, associations, and interpretations. These interactions powerfully demonstrate mind, but the question remains: Behind the fabric woven by so much functioning, is there actually any director or boss? It does not seem possible that such a complex, multi-faceted process could operate without some kind of strong central director. But if there is one, we might well wonder: who assigned this person such an all-controlling role?

11

Questioning the Foundation

When we have problems, we usually point to an external cause or search for reasons. At a deeper level we may seek understanding by questioning our mental patterns and processes. What if instead we look more closely at the foundation of our being and question mind itself? We soon discover that we can only touch the thoughts and images that constitute the surface level of mind. What lies behind, above, beyond, beneath or inside this mind remains a mystery.

Mind may have designed its processes to fit its customer—the individual 'I', but it seems indifferent to the emotional turmoil its processes can inflict on that 'I'. We may be so frustrated that we can imagine smoke coming out of our ears, yet mind keeps grinding away, its inner workings concealed by a barrier we cannot penetrate. We feel the power of mind in the pressure building inside our heads and the surge of emotion within our bodies. Mind responds to what we feel; it

Questioning the Foundation

may even be speaking to itself in ways we do not understand. But it is not necessarily giving us solutions. At this point, it is doubtful that we could trust what it says.

Meeting the Walls of Mind

Mind is rarely silent; its mumbling continues even in quiet times or during contemplation. Whatever thoughts and feedback mind presents are expressed in the phrases of the language mind has custom-made for us. But if mind should happen to lapse into silence after all, we come up against the walls of mind, the blind alleys and blank places that indicate there is nothing beyond.

It can be easy to settle down in those quiet places. If we are following some kind of spiritual discipline, we may feel that we have attained the peaceful state we have been seeking. But however remarkable these places may seem, however welcome and refreshing, they too are within the realm of dualistic mind. We are not necessarily learning anything new: Mind is still mind, and the peace we are now enjoying may vanish in the blink of an eye. We might not even remember it.

We want to make direct contact with mind itself. But we cannot. We have only the tools that

I A Fresh Look at Mind

mind has provided—the language and projections that mind can recognize and interpret. When we look for mind directly, we find nothing we can grasp or connect to. We can only engage the secondary level of perception, where the essential pronouncements have already been made. All the labels are already there, as if the knower has a dictionary ready to consult. Even after the primary interpretation has been rendered and a name applied, the senses continue their urgings, as if marketing their wares to a hesitating buyer. "How about this one, or perhaps that one instead?" Sometimes we say yes and other times no, but the process continues, repeating the same cycles.

This way of exercising mind is circular; once it begins, it has no ending. Yet we keep going, led by hopes and wishes, trusting in mind's sense of right and wrong to determine what we should do. Fascinated by what might be coming up next, fearful of what might be chasing us from behind, our minds spin round like dogs chasing their tails.

This ultimately aimless activity seems to characterize much of human experience. Whatever image or sound the senses present, whatever smell, taste, bodily sensation, thought, or emotion comes up, we generally go along with it, enjoy-

Questioning the Foundation

ing an imagined sense of freedom while following mind and senses like cows grazing on a hillside. Although time may pass pleasantly enough, if we pay close attention, we might sense a tiresome, dull quality clouding consciousness, depressing energy and eroding interest. Time slips away, and memory fades. Looking back, there may be very little we can remember.

From time to time, many among us do question the purpose of it all and wonder if there could be a better way. This question has inspired major changes in lifestyle, jobs, location, or partners. While such novelty gives hope that things will be different, without serious introspection and commitment to self-understanding, mind continues much the same. Attitudes and patterns regroup and new cycles of futility and discontent begin, with no clear path to lasting satisfaction.

We like to think that we have the freedom to be and think as we wish, but it could be that all our responses have been prepared for us, and we are just acting them out. It is as if the gun is already loaded, perhaps with the wrong ammunition. Not knowing the proper target, we shoot at random, sometimes wounding ourselves in the process.

Going along with the regime of mind, we may be unable to distinguish between what has last-

I A Fresh Look at Mind

ing value and what is transient and unreliable, wasteful, enervating, and ultimately destructive. At best, we walk through life diminished, unable to access the full dimensionality of our human consciousness. At worst, we may find ourselves entrapped in a mind cut off from all sources of happiness, committed to patterns likely to produce hostility and paranoia.

Just as each horse has its own gait, each person has his or her own way of thinking. But all thinking goes through the mechanisms of mind. So the question comes back, again and again: "Do we control mind, or does mind control us? Does mind own us or do we own mind?" If even raising this question is confusing, if our first impulse is to dismiss or invalidate it, it seems fair to say we do not know. Our language may not accommodate such questions well. But whatever the source of our confusion, it seems we need to act as though we are in control. Although the difficulties and dissatisfactions we experience reveal that our role is not always a happy one, we must maintain it for the sake of continuity.

Far more satisfying than pretending to have control would be to actually exercise it: to take a fresh look at mind, study the nature of its regime, and open options for operating it differently. If we

Questioning the Foundation

do not take this opportunity, mind will continue to build on patterns developed in response to conditions and absorbed into our sense of self. Relying on a regime invested in delusion, it will spin ever denser webs of interpretation, closing off alternatives and preventing us from savoring the richness of experience that is our birthright as human beings.

Can We Change?

Resentment, irritation, and agitation, anger, hatred, pain, agony and anguish—how often in our lives do such forceful negativities come and go? Their residues are deposited in consciousness and stored there like seeds that can sprout at any time. Between eruptions, they lie dormant, like fire under ashes, ready to burst into flame when the ashes are stirred.

    Time has its own rhythm: there is a time to prepare the soil, a time to plant and to nurture, and a time to celebrate the harvest. In the rhythms of time, human beings are born and manifest, each one differently. Problems arise and become more complex; life fills with obstacles that we step around with caution and fear. We accumulate all kinds of baggage that we carry with us as deeply

I A Fresh Look at Mind

ingrained patterns. Unexamined and nurtured through repetition, these patterns imprison our lives and drain them of accomplishment and joy.

We are part of the human lineage; our genes reflect the way human beings have developed through the centuries. As participants in this heritage, are we content simply to repeat the same tired routines that have brought suffering to countless past generations? While it may seem that we lack the knowledge and power to make a difference, it helps to consider that we have a duty, if only to ourselves, to recognize the misunderstandings that have slowed our progress and to acknowledge the extent of our ignorance. In doing so, we empower ourselves to shape our destiny in more positive ways. It might then be possible to manifest the full promise of a human birth and contribute this understanding to humanity. Is there a better legacy we could set in motion for the future?

At this critical juncture of time and opportunity, it is important that we understand how to manifest the joy of being. Sharing such rare and precious understanding could lead to a flowering of the human psyche that could foster inner and outer harmony for the benefit of all forms of life.

Questioning the Foundation

Even if we do not presently recognize the true nature of our embodiment, we, as people everywhere, yearn to be free. We are born free, with no obligations; we are free to conduct our lives in the present, and we are going to be free in the future. This understanding is itself a kind of liberation.

SECTION TWO

WORKING WITH THE MIND

Some of us have a meditation or contemplation practice to which we are committed. But if we practice without understanding the nature of mind, we may misinterpret what we experience, because mind is deceptive and does not reveal itself easily. That is what this section describes. But all of us can benefit from reflecting on this aspect of mind. Mind tends to give us what we look for, and following it blindly can entwine us in layers of confusion.

12

Mirrors of Mind

The ultimate role-player, mind has the power to create any object or image and report back to itself that what it has fabricated is real. Both steps in the process are necessary, for without them there could be no basis for further commentary or interpretation.

Contemplation

We can see mind's genius for fabrication when we engage in any kind of silent practice with the mind—whether we call our practice 'meditation', 'contemplation', 'insight', 'silent reflection', 'prayer' or anything else. The moment we sit down, everything necessary for this process to unfold is already in place. Mind takes a position, setting the stage and supporting the central actor, 'I'. As 'I' watches, mind carries out its business, creating shapes and expressions that mind then comments on and interprets.

Mirrors of Mind .

From its vast store of concepts, the mind in contemplation, the experience-seeker who yearns for total transcendence, brings up various expressions, moving with the 'I' to comment further, identifying, recycling, and validating its own interpretations and distinctions. When pleasurable sensations come up, mind interprets: "Yes, this is good, this is the way it should be, this is right," and we find ourselves thinking, "Now I am making progress." When the body becomes uncomfortable, mind says, "Perhaps I have been sitting long enough." Dialogues begin and interpretations and comments pass back and forth, weaving patterns through the mind that we relate to as real.

When pleasurable, ecstatic feelings arise, mind's commentaries continue, pointing out sensations and feeding back interpretations, associations, and meanings. Even when mind is lost and wandering, blanking out or following faint wisps of thought, its minding activity flows softly through awareness like a subtle undertow. We may hear mind whispering in the calm—or even the deep peace—of contemplation. Shimmering in the background, immanent in silence, it is poised to intensify its minding the instant concentration lapses. Contemplation that unfolds

II Working With the Mind

this way is not likely to penetrate the closed shell of the mind.

Contemplative practices may introduce us to aspects of mind we never before experienced so directly. Observing mind in an open, relaxed way can reveal the essential insubstantiality of thoughts, the urgent promptings that arise spontaneously, and the tendency of thoughts to wander discursively among random themes and associations. The ability to recognize these patterns may clarify how we tend to engage problems in ways that fail to bring resolution. Sooner or later, contemplation may lessen the hold of these patterns and brighten our outlook. Thinking that we have found a key to a new and fulfilling way of being, we may be inspired by a fresh sense of meaning and purpose. But can we trust our discovery? Mind is deceptive and does not reveal itself easily; it tends to give us what we look for, and this can lead us on a path that entwines us in layers of confusion.

13

Watching the Mind

A common instruction for beginning meditation or contemplation is to "watch the mind." When we sit down to follow it, we may have a sense of facing forward, anticipating some kind of experience but not knowing exactly what to expect. We may be watching thoughts or counting breaths; we may be monitoring awareness, observing what arises in mind from moment to moment. Behind the watcher, there may be the sense of another watcher watching the watcher, protecting mind from disturbances and monitoring thoughts in the way a shepherd tends sheep.

Getting Somewhere

"The way I know how to meditate is to have something to watch, something to do. So here I am, watching. The instructions say, 'observe the breath', or, 'observe mind', so that is what I am doing. But I have to do it very quietly and skill-

II Working With the Mind

fully, so thoughts don't come up and distract me. I have to watch secretly, so my mind does not notice. If I do it right, something different will come up, some kind of feeling or possibly some unusual happening. I don't know what will happen, but it must be something different. If I just keep waiting, if I just keep watching. . . . "

So we watch with a stealthy or sympathetic expectation, waiting for something esoteric to surprise us, something that has a different kind of flavor, something that tells us our contemplation is 'working' or suggests that we are 'getting somewhere'.

Perhaps thirty minutes pass, then forty or more. "My time is up, and I am still watching!" Then another day and another session that repeats the same pattern as before. Again watching, waiting, and looking, observing thoughts and feelings and listening to mind spin its stories. A sense of feeling arises; thoughts come, then possibly stirrings of emotion. Language comes in more strongly, interpreting these thoughts: "Now I see: contemplation means this, contemplation means that, I need to watch, I need to be aware . . . ."

Subtle currents of dialogues, sensations, and interpretations run through all this activity,

Watching the Mind

rolling together and towing us along in a gentle yet mesmerizing flow that generates a sense of momentum. Words and comments bounce back and forth within mind, spinning out dialogues and interpretations and weaving them into stories. Using our own words, speaking to us with our own voice, mind relates its stories, telling us what is going on and responding to our questions as if addressing another person. It busies itself with inner dialogues: one mind talks and another mind responds, producing a stream of narratives that provide a comforting sense of continuity and intimacy between self and mind.

Busy-ness and Blankness

Mind's dialogues draw us in, inviting participation. When they trail away, other thoughts drift by and more dialogues begin, back and forth, mind to mind. Some exchanges seem intense and serious, and we may find ourselves straining to listen, perhaps to identify who is speaking to whom and who is responding. Others are less energetic thoughts that tend to recycle the same bits of conversation over and over again.

This busy-ness of mind may dim at times, but it reemerges through periods of inner silence

II Working With the Mind

and blankness. It may seem as if someone were listening and judging in the background, ready to comment and interpret further or involve us in entirely new streams of thought. While we are quiet, mind is still observing and commenting: "Yes, I am meditating." "Now I am observing my mind." "Now I am watching out for thoughts." "Now I am watching myself watching out for thoughts." When our vigilance lapses, mind prompts us back to awareness: "Look here, look there, do this, do not do that." If it is drawn into a passing thought, it may elaborate on it until it discovers its distraction, corrects itself and regains its focus.

So many times, so many sessions, so many weeks, months, and years, yet we may still be waiting, looking, and watching. There may be times when frustration breaks through: "I can't stand all this watching and waiting! I don't seem to be getting anywhere. But I don't know what else to do!" Exactly what am I watching? While we are waiting for something to happen, are we noticing what is actually happening? Mind is directing us, casting up thoughts, repeating instructions, ordering where to look and what to do. So are we watching mind, or is mind watching us? Who is watching whom?

Watching the Mind

Although practicing with these questions in mind offers a window into the workings of mind that would otherwise pass undetected among the distractions of daily life, within the stream of mental activity, its real purpose may be overlooked and its benefits lost. Mind keeps pointing ahead, deflecting attention from itself by holding out hope for the fulfillment of vague expectations that seem just out of reach. Despite ourselves, the focus of our watching shifts almost imperceptibly from watching mind at work to following its dictates.

Boredom

Why does mind become bored? Because we are looking in the wrong direction—we're looking at where mind is pointing, rather than at the source of the pointing itself. Why? Perhaps we have not yet recognized that we could step back from mind and observe it in this way. Yet, that is what the instruction "watch the mind" is directing us to do: watch mind, take note of its tricks, and track its twists and turns. The moment language comes into contemplation, mind's regime comes into play, and that is the point where we should pay attention. We do not need to let this

II Working With the Mind

illusion-creating mind be the master. We might even ask, "Who is telling me to do this?"

As watcher, mind still has a strong authoritative role to play. Even if we become highly skilled watchers, it is likely that sensing, or cognition, or mind itself is still playing subtly within the realm of mind. If so, mind is not yet free from its dualistic subject/object orientation. As long as we hold fast to this orientation, we will continue to play within the theater of mind, rather than observing mind itself.

14

Silence and Awareness

There are times when we are engaged in contemplative practices that we may experience periods of silence, when mind seems to let go of its usual way of minding. Directed to be calm and silent, mind may welcome the opportunity to slip into a relaxed, somewhat sleepy state. At first there may be a pleasurable sense of relief as tension melts and mind becomes quiet. For a time, thoughts may come and go peacefully, like soft clouds drifting through the sky. But if we sink more deeply into a blank 'not knowing' place, mind and senses can become so still and numb that thoughts and feelings simply cease to arise. At that point, we might enter the mental equivalent of a black hole, where nothing seems to be happening.

Nothingness

We may rest in this sense of 'nothingness' a long while, immersed in a deep silence undisturbed

II Working With the Mind

by thoughts or any other kind of mental or sensory activity. There may be little or no awareness of our body or surroundings, not even a sense that time is passing. When we emerge from that state, however, what is the sum total of our experience? Nothing; a silent, negative nothing that seems the opposite of the awakened clarity we might have been expecting.

Later, when we reflect on this experience, we may be surprised to find that mind has nothing to report, interpret, or even understand. Even so, we may find ourselves thinking, "I was there, I was contemplating, and there was a flow of experience." Mind tracks back, compares the experience with our expectations and reports: "Yes, something was happening; there was a certain feeling—it was very deep, or maybe open, a sense of something—something perhaps profound, but nothing I can remember or describe."

Mind may take this further, "I must have experienced something—what was really going on? It was sort of—silent—dark—comforting, in a way, or warm. I don't have words for it, but I was meditating. I'm sure there was something happening."

Practitioners swayed by their expectations may conclude, "I had a very good session; there

Silence and Awareness

were no distractions, not even thoughts. I was meditating the whole time! I am committed to this practice; it is deeply relaxing and refreshing and I have a sense of progress and fulfillment. I want to experience this every day!"

Quieting Mind

Quieting or calming the mind in this way is the basis for most meditative disciplines, especially those practiced in the West. This kind of contemplation eases the restless hunger of the grasping mind. It relieves the sense of need; it allows consciousness to rest in silence for extended periods of time, secure and protected from pain and emotion. Practitioners learn to detach from conceptual activity; if thoughts come, they are ignored.

This approach has benefits: it gives shelter, peace, and a sense of ease and confidence in one's embodiment. It offers some respite from the pressures of stressful lifestyles and promotes physical and emotional health. Practitioners become calm and relaxed, less driven by desire and anxiety.

Those who practice for these reasons may see no purpose in analyzing the nature of their experience or investigating the possibility of access-

II Working With the Mind

ing a more vibrant, energized state of being. But there is something static in this way of being, and practitioners could spend a long time in this dull, silent place. The mind's patterns of identity, recognition, and associations may be put on hold for a time, but they tend to regroup. All too soon, the back-and-forth movements of the dualistic mind revive the operation of self and other. The subject 'I' acts on the object, likes and dislikes come into play, judgments are made, and our mind-created reality unfolds as before. Unaware of possibilities for transcending these subtle deceptions of the dualistic mind, even experienced practitioners may not realize the outcome they seek.

To ensure a different outcome, we need a completely different operation, founded on a mind that is clear and undivided, free of its present dependence upon identity, perception, language, and the sense of self. But until there is a basis for understanding how this might work, the ability to introduce it is limited.

Paying Attention

For some of us, contemplative practice may focus on becoming 'aware'. We give ourselves a very important task to accomplish through practice:

Silence and Awareness

"I need to work with my mind—I have to focus carefully, so my mind will not be distracted; I have to be aware and mindful." We proceed gently and quietly, feeling for what we sense is the right quality of contemplation, sensitively holding just the right position, as if we were balancing heavy jugs of water on our heads. "Be careful! Don't disturb the mind! Pay attention—maintain contemplation." Instructions take over, governing us, telling us what to do. Our minds become tense, compelled to echo these directives. "Be aware! Be sharp! Be clear! Focus on the instructions. Mastery comes through following instructions!"

Instructions are necessary to provide a certain level of guidance and encouragement. But since they arise within our familiar conceptual realm, they are readily appropriated by the operations of mind's regime, which repeats them at ever more subtle levels: "Be mindful! You will get lost! Be alert! Mind will fool you. Be vigilant! You may be doing the wrong thing." Even when mind seems to fall silent, it is subliminally whispering and admonishing: "Do this, don't do that, this is all right, you may do this." We do our best to stay aware, listening for whispers in the background. We become keenly aware of our senses, our ears very sensitive and alert, like deer.

II Working With the Mind

Awareness as a Goal

Some of us feel a strong need to adhere to this kind of approach. If we believe that awareness is the ultimate goal, we may tend to focus strongly on the need to be aware, even striving to be aware of being aware. Yet the need to be ready at all times to beat back intrusive thoughts and sensory perceptions holds us firmly caught in a subject/object orientation.

But it may seem we have no choice—we have to maintain the relationship between 'I' and 'my' mind. "Be aware!". . . so we do not make mistakes. "Be aware!" . . . so no one can steal our concentration, so no distractions can come up. Some element of attachment, a sense of identity or possession, is at work, influencing mind and perceptions. We are still bonded, strongly tied to a mind that is functioning on the level of identification.

For those new to contemplation, this focused way of watching mind can be a useful training. But it is difficult to say whether it can actually lead toward liberating mind. The ability to trace the process of cognition and the interactions of thoughts and senses may not be sufficient to free ourselves of mental and emotional obscurations. To penetrate and eliminate subtle and persistent

Silence and Awareness

afflictions, it is necessary to take clarity beyond the level of possession so that it becomes indestructible.

Meditation, prayer, and contemplative practices can relieve pain and lessen our burden of suffering without being sufficient to quiet the business of mind. When we identify with our practice, we tend to project our own expectations and concepts into the meditation experience and set ourselves above or apart from it. Mind understands and supports this position, prompting us to take control. For instance, we find ourselves thinking, "I can tell the difference between a good practice and one that does not work for me." Again, mind may cast the self as the beneficiary of contemplation, prompting other thought experience: "Oh, I like this feeling! This is great! This is it!"

15

The Problem with Ownership

Because the sense of ownership arises automatically as soon as mind labels a perception, it can be difficult to avoid it, whether we focus on the inner workings of mind or on external objects. Awareness of an object activates the polarity of the dualistic mind, compelling mind to establish the object's position. Responding to a "longing to belong," mind posits a subject: the notion of 'I'. In this single step, mind validates 'I' as subject and me as owner: "This object belongs to me," "this object is mine." Wherever 'I' manifests, ownership appears also.

Having created this product, mind tends to follow up as if we were customers it wished to satisfy. Encouraging thoughts may come: "I had wonderful insights—truly blissful feelings, I felt on top of the world! I can tell I'm getting into this practice; I can sense it in my body and my feelings. I have a very satisfying sense of fulfillment.

The Problem with Ownership

Before, I felt so conflicted and frustrated, but now I am feeling more confident and 'together'. Thoughts are not pressuring me so much and my positive feelings are more intense. I feel less agitated, more relaxed, more in touch with myself. I am having many good experiences, so I must be making progress. This is definitely worth doing!"

I as Customer, Owner, Benefactor

From this perspective, 'I' am not only the customer who collects and seeks to own experiences, but also the benefactor and recipient, the one who gives him- or herself the benefits of contemplation. 'I' am also the one who profits from it, the one looking for something better with every session. Many individuals engage their practice in this way: "This is my spiritual journey, my true home, and I am committed to it. I am getting tangible benefits, and I am proud of what I have accomplished. It gives me a sense of peace and fulfillment Nothing else engages me in the same way. I have to have it."

Such thoughts motivate practitioners and encourage them with positive expectations. When an experience gives us pleasure or satisfaction, we tend to identify with the activity that pro-

II Working With the Mind

duced it, so it seems natural to consider a spiritual practice as our personal possession. In time, this approach to practice can take on a quality of compulsion—we have to do it. That is why the motivation is effective.

Ownership can also exclude and separate: "I deserve these rich feelings, because I have a long-standing investment in my practice. Others do not have the same kind of investment in their own path. I am more protected and secure, so I do not have to go through the same hardships as they do. I understand what they are going through, but I am not necessarily involved that way anymore."

When these kinds of thoughts come up, it helps to realize that our positive results are being undermined by the mind's insistence that the benefits 'belong to me'. That is the nature of mind; that is where we are. We cannot yet stand on anything better.

When 'me', 'myself', and 'my experience' are central to our perspective, we may feel a strong need to protect them. If we lack awareness of what is happening, we may cling tightly to this me-centered realm, which wraps around us like an impenetrable shell. Now we have locked away

The Problem with Ownership

everything that contemplation would normally nourish: a sense of the wonder of being, an open, receptive attitude, and awareness. Even after practicing various methods and techniques and taking many classes, programs, and retreats, even after a long spiritual journey, this may be where we end up.

So sad and limiting, this sense of ownership that separates and isolates! Sad because we will have to struggle a long time before we can let it go. Sad, also, because we cannot manifest and share the true benefits of contemplation.

However we name our method of practice, as long as it involves mind, tendencies toward ownership are likely to emerge. If we allow mind to nurture them, the result will most likely be misunderstanding and disappointment.

16

Getting What We Look For

"But, wait! Before I started this kind of practice, I had lots of problems. Now I have had a peak experience—the ultimate, most blissful experience imaginable! My whole perspective has changed! I have truly opened to love."

Yes, sometimes spiritual experience awakens a very deep devotion that can focus on our concept of God or spirituality, on humanity, on specific persons, or on symbols or other kinds of objects. We are enraptured, as if we had fallen deeply in love. We are totally convinced: "This is what I have been looking for! I am happy, I feel fulfilled. My life is perfect just as it is!"

Many practitioners have peak experiences, especially in the early stages of their practice. But this, too, takes place in the realm of mind. We may have been anticipating a certain kind of experience, and now our mind is accommodating us in the way we expected. While we may feel that we have attained what we were yearning for, what we have actually attained may only be a satisfying relationship with our own experience.

Mind has the power to express itself in many ways. From one moment to the next, it can arouse passion, love, or joy, or possibly their opposites—dullness, anger, crushing disappointment and dissatisfaction. In its positive modes, mind can congratulate itself: "Look! See what wonderful feelings I can give you! You could wish for nothing better! This is such a great method, such a powerful technique!" Yes, but we have to remember that all kinds of expressions—positive, negative, and neutral—are manufactured by mind. The seller is mind, the customer 'I' is mind, the expression is mind. And mind goes to negative places as well as to happier ones.

The real problem is that this mind is not likely to go where it has not been before. However ecstatic our experience, it is likely that we are still within the illusion-making realm of mind.

At any point, with any practice, if we become attached to our accomplishments and hold on to them, we may not be able to recognize and deal with the real enemies that are blocking our path.

II   Working With the Mind

This is a serious obstacle. Whatever we may feel we have achieved, this is not the place to stop. Instead, we can take a fresh look at our observations of mind. Are we unknowingly falling into the very patterns of self-deception we had hoped to transcend? We can check to see if we are holding tightly to a position, or if there is a subtle— or perhaps even obvious—self-orientation. We can note whether we are observing in a detached manner or are rewinding and repeating our own experience. Are we experiencing just what we expected? If so, are we grasping the experience or feeling possessive of it?

It is important to understand that we get what we look for, and our expectations of where to look and how to look may mislead us. Mind is only too ready to point in the wrong direction. For instance, when mind and body grow restless or cause trouble, we may escape for a time into the peace and silence of contemplation, and mind may support this move with a gratifying sense of accomplishment. But eventually we have to come back to the same situation. Have we looked in the right place?

Facing Obstacles Directly

The only way to be free is to clear our mind of all residues of grasping and identity. We can begin by taking advantage of opportunities to investigate what lies behind our anger, anxiety, frustration, guilt, and other manifestations of negativity. When these patterns come up, we can lighten up the urge to escape and turn to face the troubling thought or emotion directly. We can pronounce its name, examine it, study it intently, and bring it closer and closer to us. When there is nothing between us and the perception, just seeing, with no associations or interpretations, the focus of our attention will open up, and its character will change.

Since these patterns come up naturally within the operations of the dualistic mind, we may need to confront them many times. But eventually they will weaken, and in time may not come up at all. We might regard this as a way to immunize ourselves from the tyranny of mind's regime. As we gain confidence and certainty, the force of grasping and identity will weaken, and we will not be thrust so easily into painful situations. In time, we become stable, free of negativity, able to transform obstacles as they arise.

II Working With the Mind

For this we do not necessarily need a special situation, a complex system of practice, visualizations, or direction. Any time obstacles come up, we can be warriors, without fear. When we practice with this understanding, obstacles can become our partners, our friends, our energy, our wisdom, and our path, for we will have a different way to deal with them.

17

Cutting Through Mind-Business

Contemplation is intended to free us from the pressures of self-image and obligations, from ego and emotions, and from the limitations and distortions that result from conceptualization. The aim is to allow mind to rest on neutral ground, free from assumptions and associations that support self-oriented views.

If we have such expectations, we may be willing to work patiently with all the mind-business that drifts through our contemplation. But this is like cutting through a very thick jungle one tangle of vines at a time. We watch thoughts, wrestle with pros and cons, push and pull with likes and dislikes, notice weaknesses and needs for improvement, follow interpretations and trains of thought. Since such 'mind policing' interferes with contemplation, we may feel we need to intensify our efforts to concentrate. But the more effort we put into observing mind, the more active and agitated it becomes, so that pressure builds up. We may become frustrated and discouraged, either thinking that contemplation is too much work or else blaming ourselves when we sense we are not getting a good 'result'. But this frustration may be difficult to acknowledge. If someone asks, "Is your understanding of mind improving," the answer is likely to be, "Of course. I am genuinely involved in this practice, watching and analyzing mind."

Understanding the Acquisitive 'Customer Mind'

If we are frustrated and restless, preoccupied with right and wrong, shoulds and woulds, and other judgmental distinctions, we are undermining our own efforts. Instead of just allowing thoughts to come and go, we are watching and evaluating the process, absorbed in the details and making adjustments according to our understanding of the 'right' and 'wrong' ways to observe the mind. We are still playing the customer, engaging the business of mind. This too can be viewed as a form of understanding: understanding what practitioners do in tracking the business of mind, understanding how mind labels, how it makes meaning, and how it plays games. Both kinds of discipline—contemplation of mind and analysis of its mechanisms—have value. But they also have limitations.

The Lure of Getting Somewhere

If mind eventually grows calmer and our outlook more positive, we may feel that we are getting the benefits we expected from our investment of time and energy in contemplative practice. If our practice also rewards us with pleasurable experiences, mind can become very attached to this seductive flow of feeling. This may trigger another round of expectations. We may be following instructions, proceeding correctly in our practice, but mind may anticipate some greater reward that is just out of reach, a prize that entices us to intensify our efforts. We do not necessarily know what it is, but we feel compelled to reach for it, because mind is telling us, "I need it, I want it." Mind's tendency to push toward resolution impels us to strive toward our goal.

Conceptual formulations that involve pointing out and naming—even the communication necessary to receive instructions—can take us far away from contemplation. The tendency is contemplation—is limited by its dependence on the conceptualizing aspect of mind. Of the fully open, 360 degree knowledge that is theoretically possible, we are accessing only a tiny arc, possibly no more than a single degree. Until we become more attuned to the full dimensionality of mind, we have to confine ourselves to that tiny space and carry out our business within it.

Closed Circuitry of Mind

What can we know of the zone beyond the 'red light'? We could speculate that the territory beyond concepts means a state where mind is 'empty' of concepts. But this is self-defeating. Now we are labeling this unknown territory with a known label: 'emptiness'. We are establishing it as a concept and pointing out how it is to be interpreted. We seem to be involved in contradiction.

Similarly, as we identify, name, and explain such spiritually significant words as enlightenment, wisdom, and realization, we fall into our familiar dualistic patterns of discourse. Intent on enabling mind to interpret their meanings, we accept the meanings mind provides, forgetting that they are simply concepts provided by a mind

Obeying the Parameters

unable to function beyond its dualistic subject/object framework.

As long as we focus on the objects that appear within the limited framework of mind, we are seeing only part of the whole picture. Knowledge based on this partial picture seems to be little more than a special kind of guesswork—guesses presented by language that has been constructed by mind. That is why, when we use concepts that point out an alternative to 'ordinary' mind, it seems especially important that we maintain an internal system of checks and balances. Instead of accepting what mind presents, we should remind ourselves to question: "Who is judging? Who is evaluating? Who is observing and pointing out?" Isn't it our 'ordinary' concept-bound mind?

For our knowledge to be complete, we need something more. We need to know its origin and how it connects with the perception and minding processes that are facets of mind's regime. We need to be aware of the framework, the pointer, the act of pointing, and what is being pointed out.

19

Closing Access to Awareness

In all aspects of our lives, we would benefit greatly from knowing the full context of our thoughts and actions. But mind's dedication to identifying and interpreting hijacks our awareness and robs us of the clarity we need to broaden our perspective in this manner.

Mind's need to identify and move on makes it impatient with questions that penetrate more incisively. As a result, if we are asked to investigate this 'I' that is observing and pointing out, this 'I' that needs to establish connections, we may become frustrated, unable to grasp the purpose of such an unfamiliar kind of question. But we do have some options. If we observe our perceptions, noting the point where 'this is' shifts to 'what this means to me', we may see how quickly mind diverts awareness away from simple observation into meanings and interpretations.

If we can sustain our focus on the questions that penetrate mind's constructs, we might find

Closing Access to Awareness

ourselves thinking, "That is an interesting perspective. I would very much like to know more about how this works." But this can be another point of deception. We may feel our mind waiting expectantly, gathering information, trying to point out what is happening, but not quite able to identify the concepts and associations that match it.

Straining for Resolution

At such times we may feel as though our mind is temporarily on hold. It is clearly active, but unable to formulate the concepts that would express what is happening. We may be trying to grasp a concept or experience a state of being that we have only imagined, heard, or read about. We may be keenly aware of straining after something, anxious to improve something or to present ourselves well, but something seems to be preventing resolution. If we pride ourselves on having a quick, responsive intelligence, we may be startled to note the dull, sluggish quality of inertia that has suddenly come over our mind.

Even in contemplation, the business of the mind creates a jungle of complexities that fill the clear openness of mind with the anxiety of grasping and self-doubt. Pointing ahead, mind pushes

II Working With the Mind

us to keep going, but at the same time it piles up obstacles in our path. We may be yearning for clarity and a sense of respite from all this minding, yet the pressure to go forward only agitates the mind further. The dialogues continue . . . .

"This is not what I am looking for. Contemplation should not be like this. I still have a problem, but I should not have a problem. Perhaps I should shift my position or try breathing differently. Just sitting here waiting for something isn't working for me. I'm feeling kind of sleepy, blanking out, getting a little cold and numb. Maybe I'll just lie down for a while."

When we reach such an impasse, our choices are limited. We can continue on in the same way as best we can, or we can give up. But neither one seems right. Searching for answers within its own realm, using the tools of language, words, and imagination, the mind comes back to the same place it began. Frustrated, we may ask ourselves, "Why is this happening?"

Mind has a way of recoiling back in on itself, gathering perceptions, concepts, associations, and meanings and feeding them back to mind. While we feel we are moving forward, looking for something that seems just on the verge of

Closing Access to Awareness

appearing, we may be experiencing a feedback system that is actually moving backwards, sideways, or inward. Perhaps we are simply listening to mind mumbling to itself.

Looking from this perspective, can we consider a different way to view what is happening? We can understand that mind is reading what mind presents; we know that mind is interpreting, then receiving back its own interpretations, which are once again presented, expanded, received back, and reinterpreted. If this insight arises in contemplation, it may indicate that we are becoming aware of the closed circuitry that governs the operations of mind.

II Working With the Mind

It may be difficult to accept that the very structures that appear to support the basic sanity and competence of the mind can subvert its intrinsic urge for freedom and transcendence. Thus, when we discover these patterns through contemplation or experience the deflecting and re-directing tricks of mind's regime, we may find it difficult to investigate further. How else can we explain why are we so easily discouraged from venturing into fresh landscapes of mind, where its regime cannot function the same way?

Like victims everywhere, we tend to identify with our tormentors. We depend on them for our sense of reality—for our state of mind, our understanding, our relationships and interactions—for all that constitutes our being as we know it. We are totally, completely dedicated to the order they have established.

But do we understand what lies past the horizons established by the regime? Can we say how strongly the fabric is woven? Will it hold up under all experiences that life presents? What beauty, what fresh vistas might reveal themselves beyond the borders that now confine our being? These are the kinds of questions to carry into contemplation, to be asked every time we come up against the walls of mind.

21

Understanding the Inner Story

Do we understand how mind knows mind? Have we any evidence that reveals how mind talks to mind? Mind talking to mind is a story, just as our life is a story. What else could it be? A hundred years from now, no one will consider our lives as anything more than stories. Yet our lives are important to us and we take them very seriously. So why not pay serious attention to the stories that mind tells?

When we dream, especially if we have dreams that are vivid, do we think they are real? Or do we think of them as stories told by our mind? We could be imagining—recording various versions of a story with all manner of characters, qualities, and interactions that produce different feelings and emotions. Are our memories of dreamstories like that? Do we remember effortlessly creating such stories and living within them, as if we were taking a journey that had many interesting twists and turns? Now we are creating a

II Working With the Mind

similar kind of story—the story of our waking life—and relating to it as real. Could we be playing a secret trick on ourselves?

If our life really unfolds within the realms of imagination, our judgments and reactions to what is happening are equally imaginary. Yet that is not how we engage them. As our minds interpret our experience from different perspectives, we are happy, we are excited; we are apprehensive, fearful, unhappy. We record all the dramas and narratives that move through the mind. We hear them, we accept and establish them, and we live with them. These stories become part of our image of ourselves, our own personal history, and we respond accordingly. When they come up in memory, we say, "That's what really happened," rather than, "That is basically my imagination at work."

Even if we cannot change them—they are still our stories!—we take our stories seriously and hold on to them, because without them parts of our lives would simply disappear. If we cannot hold on to them, perhaps because others do not see them the way we do, they become irrelevant.

Whether we experience our stories as a genuine account of our lives or consider them subject

Understanding the Inner Story

to revision, the framework, content, interpretations, and significance of these stories is taking place in the mind—nothing else is happening. We cannot necessarily catch it happening, but the story takes us over and becomes part of us.

Caught up in the movements of our mind, separated from our being, our life is a story. We live in a story. We are part of a story. We are the story. We contribute to it and take on its attributes. We are the one who orchestrates, responds, and interacts with it, accepting that this is the way our story goes. We have nothing else other than our story: our version of any experience is our story. Everything we receive and project is yet another part of the story.

When we come to understand that we are in the story too, projecting, receiving, interpreting, and showing off the results within the echo chambers of mind, we not only begin to see how the mind works, but also we get a fresh glimpse of freedom. We start to see certain patterns, and recognize them for what they are. Sometimes we get carried away with a topic and elaborate on it. At other times we do not remember exactly how we told the story earlier, but may decide we would like to revise it and present it in another

II Working With the Mind

way. Another conclusion to the story may accidentally pop up, or our memory may create a different story entirely. From time to time, we may experience a 'reality-check' made necessary by hearing someone else's version or interpretation of the story, and we may reinterpret the story to give it a new focus and believability.

The Story of Contemplation

So, are the fruits of contemplation part of our story? The structure seems very similar. We have an experience in meditation, or perhaps in prayer, and say, "I love it, it is mine, this is how mind is supposed to be." But the only thing we can accurately say is "I did not understand what was happening."

This is not a criticism, but an important acknowledgement of reality. When we recognize that we have not understood, we also acknowledge that there is something to be understood. If we consider carefully what this means, we may glimpse the possibility of a new and creative way of understanding,

Our ordinary way of knowing, shaped within the regime of mind, is linear and flat, relatively devoid of the vital dynamic of creativity and

Understanding the Inner Story

revelation. When the mind points to an object and we recognize it, it is because we understand the labels and the meaning, all of which are products of the past. When all the labels and associations have been properly arranged, we may weave more thoughts about the object or experience into our story. While this follows the reality-rules established by mind, this is only one way of enriching our story. There are other ways we have yet to explore, and some have the potential to penetrate the all-encompassing envelope of mind.

In this light, it is possible to re-interpret mind's signals to turn back when the borders of conceptual construction loom before us as an invitation to proceed. Acknowledging that we do not understand gives mind pause: its minding operations are briefly put on hold, allowing glimpses of a new, more liberated way of understanding—one that does not require that clever person in the background of our minds to take on the endless task of interpretation.

22

Seeds of Separation

We are convinced we each have individual minds, but at a fundamental level, mind seems to be a uniform entity. It has certain properties that appear to be fixed, it makes use of the same basic systems of perception and cognition, and it plays the same games, no matter what individual happens to be operating it. However we might like to think that these systems and games do not apply to us, or that they apply to us in a different way, when we examine mind more closely, we find that we may be looking at the same fundamental entity, no matter who claims ownership.

Then why are people so different? Here we can offer a story. Imagine that a long time ago, no one danced. Then one day, one person, then a second and a third, began moving in a way others found pleasing, and more and more people began making the same movements. At first, dancing was all gesture and movement, but over time,

Seeds of Separation

someone began to beat a drum; the rhythm of the drum brought the group together and added meaning to the gestures. As others were inspired to elaborate and improvise, more and more people began dancing and playing drums. Specific styles developed, distinguished by different steps and rhythms and creative combinations. Perhaps strong preferences developed, or certain styles took on unique associations and were favored by specific groups, classes, or tribes. In time, many styles of dancing came into being in response to different contexts and purposes. Is it possible that the mental patterns that make us unique may have developed in similar ways?

Foundation for Misunderstanding

While we may have the same human mind and the same basic operating system, individual minds can run different programs that are not necessarily compatible. After all, when individual minds view the same picture, they do not necessarily arrive at the same understanding of what the image represents.

Since mind instinctively reshapes perceptions to accord with what has been identified previously, what is obvious and right from our perspec-

II Working With the Mind

tive may not be true for others. If rigid patterns of reaction set in, with no way to accommodate opposing views, the result can be confusion, disagreements, heightened emotions, grudges, and peace-destroying hatred.

Even when everyone uses the same words, the connotations of these words can vary widely. For a time, two individuals may seem to be thinking the same way, but eventually differences in meaning and valuation become obvious, and they sense the separation. Such differences manifest most strongly among societies and cultures, but they also show up between individuals, complicating communication, fostering misunderstanding, and sowing seeds of conflict.

We can see from the state of our world today that such patterns of misunderstanding have universal significance to humanity. If they take firm root in the mind, they can persist through many generations and give rise to countless forms of suffering. Unless we can understand how mind operates, so that we can defuse potential conflicts at their root, confusion will only increase. And such is the power of mind that the consequences of confusion are likely to become ever more severe.

23

Validating the Validator

There is.

With these words we state that something is real or exists in some manner. 'There' is a symbol pointing to something that has been established, and 'is' indicates that what is being pointed to exists. 'There is' indicates immediate recognition of a perception, thought, or fact that is now confirmed and validated.

Prior to validation, the conditions for identifying a perception have already been established, but the entity is not yet recognized, like an egg that has been laid but not yet hatched. This 'prior' state is an unknown territory. We do not know how it came to be or what conditions apply to it; we assume it exists, because in retrospect we know that a perception is immanent, but we have no way of knowing for certain. It would seem to be 'our territory', but we do not know how to enter it or communicate with it. How can

II Working With the Mind

we validate what we cannot grasp and recognize? We need a witness.

In response to this, the answer comes: "Mind can validate itself!" It seems that mind has a spokesman, an interpreter or intermediary who knows our language and reassures us: "The realm of mind is not chaotic or accidental; everything is in order and ready to go. There are labels prepared for everything conceivable and for their characteristics, associations, and history as well. There are senses endowed with sensitivity; there are perceptions, identity, labeling and recognition—a whole regime. There are interactions and movement of meanings, feelings, and emotions. There is language to ensure that everything is correctly identified and that there is no mistake. Everything has been taken care of. There it is—there is reality. These are the tools for operating it. What you do with it from here is up to you."

The Realm of 'There Is'

Every time we say 'there is', we not only point something out, we also point out what we are doing: "I am perceiving, identifying, characterizing and possessing. I am connecting my personal, subjective awareness to the condition,

Validating the Validator

quality, and meaning of my observation. I am acting on my need to establish connections and hold on to them."

For instance, if mind's pronouncement, 'there is', points to a perception that accords with mind's pre-established notion of anger, mind will identify anger, call up agitation as the appropriate response, and embellish it with associations and feelings. Almost immediately, anger becomes real; body and mind respond, and we cannot stop emotions from flowing. As mind continues to identify and label each element in this unfolding chain of events, language comes more strongly into play, contributing reasons and justifications that spark more interactions, dialogues, and commentaries and summon memories that may carry a strong emotional charge.

From this point, mind could continue to spin out any number of stories that point in different directions. But now we want to turn mind around and track its stories to their origin instead. We want to know the history of this anger and validate for ourselves the reality that provoked it.

Is there a structure we can trace that allows us to do this? Again, we meet the interpreter. "Mind has already created a history for you and

II Working With the Mind

the regime of mind is now presenting it to you in ways you can understand. You have the appropriate responses, the thoughts, expressions, and behavior expected of you. This is the process that you have learned to engage and carry out. Beyond that, there is nothing that you can grasp or express, so there is no point in analyzing further."

We need to know more about what underlies this process, but we cannot seem to obtain that information. We can only accept what mind has presented. If mind has interpreted what we are feeling as anger, we can only hope that the anger, perhaps now escalating to rage, will not drive us to actions we will later regret. But we are beginning to see how easily this can happen.

How far can we investigate the significance of 'there is'? We can look to the senses, and we can give reasons for what we feel, think, and do. Sometimes we can connect cause and effect and arrive at explanations that provide some degree of satisfaction. But going deeper, we meet with a barrier we cannot penetrate. Beyond it is where the interpreter retreats when we ask who validates the reality of our experience.

The realm beyond 'there is' appears to have a unique sort of system that we cannot see or

Validating the Validator

touch. We can only accept the answer that the interpreter proffers: "Reality is validated by consensus. Everyone agrees to what is." Pressed further, the interpreter balks: "Anything more is impossible to know or express. The question is irrelevant and of no consequence." It appears that we are now at a dead end.

This is a very fruitful place to proceed with our inquiry. We would like to know how the mechanism of validation works, how it produces meaning instantly and coherently, almost magically, from whatever takes place in that 'prior' territory we cannot access. But our present understanding operates only from the point of recognition forward. We take birth in the realm of 'there is'. We live in that reality, placing great faith in 'the fact of the matter'. We own the whole operating system of existence—we wear it, we share it, and we carry it closely, playing it privately, rewinding it, then playing it again and again, as if listening to a favorite recording. But we are ignorant of its origin or composition. Wherever it takes our thoughts, feelings, and emotions, we have to cope with it. We cannot operate any other way.

24

The Reality-Realm of Mind

Sensing, feeling, and thinking, each person inhabits the realm of his or her own reality and plays very privately within it, thoroughly committed to it from birth to death. A pre-established reality is projected as an outside world, and we perceive objects and attributes: grass that is green, sky that is blue. Since everyone operates with many of the same programs of mind, we share this reality in common, adapting its perceived qualities in accord with our individual faculties. We 'upload' the reality-realm program and watch it play out again and again. Running on a loop, the program continually comments on its own operations according to its own projections. Sense-perception operates as part of the program, but since we are not aware of that mechanism, we have not formulated the concepts and language that might enable us to see how it works.

The Reality-Realm of Mind

While this description of how reality unfolds seems to go against our usual understanding, consider what happens when we dream. Conversations and interactions in dreams are a kind of inner perception, but they seem just as real as outer perceptions. Although in a dream there is no object that we can actually see, hear, smell, feel, or taste, some kind of sensory functioning is going on, even in the absence of an external cause.

What we call cognition of 'outer' reality could be said to operate the same way. In waking life as in dreams, the flow of mental imagery, private thoughts, feelings, sensing, feedback, and identity gives rise to a unique, very convincing reality that we find attractive, perhaps even seductive. Yet, this is just the functioning of mind itself— for the mind, by the mind and of the mind—as it continually rewinds, interprets, and synthesizes its own sensing and cognitive processes. The dynamic power and magnitude of our mental imagery appears able to sustain a sense of momentum that validates the reality of what is seen. After all, in dreams as in waking life, the flow of mental imagery, private thoughts, feelings, sensing, feedback, and identity weaves a unique, very convincing reality that we find attractive, perhaps even seductive.

II Working With the Mind

But if cognition is the product of mind mechanisms, what is its basis? Something must provide the continuity that impels it to operate. Whether we call it the power of mind or the power of the will, or possibly the energy we identify as sensation, something must provide the continuity of feeling that brings our experience alive. We usually have a sense of the momentum that conveys the feeling of transition to a newly emerging moment, but this may only be a side effect of another dynamic—the motion of thoughts and feelings spooling out and rewinding. We could live forever in this familiar and comfortable place, playing our reality-tapes in continuing cycles of duplication. But do we have to settle for that? Is there a better way to understand the nature of mind and its relationship to reality?

Foundation for a New Way of Action

While the natural brilliance of mind has no foreground or background, or any other sense of place, mind seems to need some point of reference in order to receive and interpret meaning from the flow of sensory impressions. Mind's way of accommodating this need has led to our dualistic way of understanding. Identifying through polarity and contrast, we focus on measurements

The Reality-Realm of Mind

that mark out the distance from here to there and create the other distinctions we rely upon, using the language of our customer minds.

When we are young, the distinctions we make may not be that complex, but as the scope of our experience expands, we add more specifics: concepts, private thoughts, memories, and personal habit patterns. Noting differences and relating to them as substantively real, we divide them into categories, assign them territories, erect walls to separate them, and place them within the walls in carefully constructed boxes. While we tend to trust 'our' experience, it is important to realize that every moment of that experience depends on such specifics. We know reality according to the way mind presents and interprets it.

As we take our study of understanding deeper, we may question who put up the walls and divided experience into all these compartments and zones. Was it the senses, thoughts, and habitual patterns that created different categories? Or could it be that language evolved that way?

If mind establishes categories as it scans our experience, isolating what seems relevant and shaping it into reality, any limitations imposed by that way of operation will mean that all our

II Working With the Mind

knowledge will be limited as well. Unless we can find ways to operate mind differently, we will continue to receive knowledge according to the structures mind creates to accommodate it.

This is the challenge that faces us. We seem to have no way to investigate mind's limitations. However certain we may be of how and why we think and feel the way we do, without being clear on the full context of all the thoughts and beliefs that have arisen in mind and been developed through the ceaseless activity of mind's regime, it is more likely that we do not know. Few of us would admit to that depth of not-knowing, but is there another choice? Does our present level of understanding enable us to us answer that question?

25

Turning Toward Clarity

If a place is unknown, how can we go there? If something is inconceivable, how can we come to understand it? We can only work with things that are known, and for the most part this means the things that everyone knows and supports. We set out on the same journey as everyone else and extend understanding in the familiar ways. Like our fellow travelers, we label, name, identify, witness, and sense, we experience feelings and make judgments. When mind decides, we accept its decision. That is the way our reality is constituted—normal, regular reality: common sense, truth. From all of these interactions, we draw conclusions that are logical, rational, and reasonable. That is our story—a story we all understand.

Virtual Reality

This may sound like a theory, but it is meant more as a description that you can validate

II Working With the Mind

for yourself. Any game we play—any story we enact—is based on the dynamic activity of mind. Mind establishes our view of time. Mind uses language to create different versions of what we know, and we understand them.

It is as if mind is dialoguing with its own internal editors, mind to mind, imagination to imagination: "So what is the problem? I understand what you understand." "All right, if you understand it, it is probably true. Do you understand it?" "Yes, if you want to say it that way, I suppose I understand what your version of the story means. Do you have any other versions?" "Yes, I may have another way to tell it." Back and forth, mind and imagination share stories with one another, adding perspectives and variations, shifting feelings somewhat as the drama unfolds.

This kind of mind-to-mind interaction encompasses all of human history. It weaves the fabric of existence within the mind, giving rise to an imitation of reality held together by interlocking networks of emotional and mental patterns. Though each aspect of the extant world demonstrates its specific transitory and contingent nature, mind's story features a permanent subject—'I'—as its central operator. Otherwise the story would not work for us.

Turning Toward Clarity

Imagine that we are telling a story to ourselves. Only we know the story; there is no other audience, and our story is not relevant to anyone else. We are observing that our mind is identifying, recognizing, and creating our reality; it is commenting on our actions, arousing feelings we can now release and let go; it is bringing up thoughts that we know will aggravate resentments and we can smile as understanding dissolves them. We are now aware of everything that comes up in mind, balancing easily in the flow of feelings and thoughts, with mind alert yet relaxed. We may feel we have arrived at the point where we have perfect understanding of mind. There is no mystery left, and we now think there is nothing else left to understand. But how do we deal with the background murmurings, the communication of mind to mind that only we can hear?

Is there anything that is not a story? So far, our minds do not seem to know of such a possibility. When does the story end? It ends when we develop the habit of looking inward, at the 'from' of our experience, and seeing mind's mechanism at work. It ends when we realize that it really is just a story.

II Working With the Mind

Going More Deeply

Clarity arises through observing mind. Observing the mechanisms of mind, seeing how they operate, what calms and what agitates them, leads to a potent understanding of mind's nature. To develop this understanding further, we can study the architecture and engineering of our mental patterns and observe how they play out in experience. Then we can see what we are involved in, how our patterns are constructed, how we assume roles and enact them, and how mind artfully positions itself as director, knower, and leader.

Understanding this much, we can go more deeply into the fundamental question, to whom does this mind belong? Our inquiry pursues this question by asking further questions: Is mind the same as 'I'? Did 'I' create mind, or did mind create 'I'? Which is mind and which is 'I'? Do 'I' belong to mind, or does mind belong to 'I'? Do 'I' understand who owns whom?

If we have not yet developed a conceptual framework for this way of exploring, these questions may seem meaningless—like the babble of children learning to talk. We may feel we are long past the stage where we could ask such questions or find it valuable to do so. But they go to the heart of what mind is, and they offer us valuable opportunities to turn assumptions upside down and think in new ways.

If we sense an inner resistance, or perhaps a willful reluctance to engage this line of questioning, we can use language and feelings to relax the regime of mind. We can dialogue with the mind. Even as mind reminds and directs us, we can encourage it to open and allow us to access to deeper levels of consciousness. Just as mind uses language to remind and direct us, we can use language and feelings to relax the regime of mind. The more we understand the nature of mind, the more calmness and clarity we can offer the mind, and the more effectively mind can serve the whole of our being.

Section Three

Mind and Time

Why are we interested in understanding time? The simple response is: "Because the regime of mind as it now operates limits our freedom and leads inexorably to suffering." That regime has become unnecessarily confining, a product of an earlier age that the dynamic power of time may have rendered obsolete. Since the model that sustains the present regime developed from mind's interaction with time—the unit of experience that allows perception to take place—we begin by looking more closely at the relationship of mind and time.

III Mind and Time

of our reality: the sense of being, the sense of surroundings, and the sense of movement 'from' and 'to'. Like a seed planted by mind in the field of time, this projection, developed and replicated throughout human history, is the model for each instant of experience. While the specifics change from moment to moment, the model is continuously replicated; it persists, unquestioned and unquestionable, perpetuating itself through the power of its own dynamic. We participate by embodying it and projecting into all we think and do.

Senses, perception, identity, re-cognition, and labeling, 'I', me, mine, interpretations and associations: Time enables mind to play all these roles. This template for reality has worked for us throughout human history. It now seems so reflexive that we may never stop to think about how it works or to investigate its implications to our thoughts and actions. It is as if we have received it as a sealed unit stamped 'do not open', As its end user, we may be able to manipulate it to deal with some of the upsets and malfunctions that arise, but it would not normally occur to us that we could safely open it up and investigate a problem's point of origin. If such a thought were to arise, would we have the confidence to investigate mind in this way? Can we try?

27

Architect of Time

If mind, time, and perception did not come together in some way, we would not have a sense of time or be able to know what is happening. In turn, perception itself is made possible by the nature of our senses and mental activity.

Prior to perception, we might think of mind as completely free of content, clear and reflective as a highly polished mirror. Then, in response to sensory activity, patterns of light and shadow begin to flicker. As they intensify and brighten into reflections, light reveals colors and texture, while other sensory impressions converge into forms, sounds, tastes, bodily sensations and fragrance. This sensory activity alerts the mind that something has presented itself for identification, and mind reaches out to grasp it, awakening the first stirrings of a quality of understanding.

In order to identify the sensory activity, mind marks out and projects a tiny unit of experience, an instant in which recognition can take place.

III Mind and Time

Let us call this instant a nanosecond, literally a billionth of a second, a unit impossibly small, but still large enough to allow for further divisions.

Having projected the nanosecond, mind recognizes what the senses have presented, identifies the object, and applies a label that seals the object's identity. But this label is not based on the initial flickering of light and shadow, for the first point of contact is already past. It arises instead from reflections that continue to develop from subsequent points of contact, as we become involved in a secondary process of remembering, re-reflecting and re-cognizing. We did not notice the point at which reflections replaced initial impressions; in fact, since the transition takes place before the label is presented and recognized, we would not even know how to notice it. Already we are trailing behind, following reflections of reflections as mind weaves the tapestry of our reality.

Sculpting Reflections into Reality

The instant mind recognizes the object, the subject appears also, brought into being by further reflections that bounce back and forth within mind. Subject and object accommodate one another, creating the environment for self and other, the dualistic perspective that characterizes our point of view and conditions our understanding of reality.

Reflections—mind reflecting to mind, mind feeding back to mind—provide the continuity necessary for sensory impressions to develop to the point where mind can generate a label that identifies the object and imprints it in memory. That label is now accepted as 'real': The object has a name, and the sound of that name can call up the image that corresponds to it. Thereafter, the identity of that object comes up instantly, because mind already knows the label appropriate to it.

Meaning and associations arise simultaneously with the label—this is red, this is soft, this is good, this is not good. Additional specifics, judgments, and interpretations follow. Instantly, we not only know the name of what has been perceived, but we can also point out the qualities and characteristics associated with that name.

Point of Recognition

The point of recognition may be infinitesimally small, but without this small interval, mind cannot identify anything. Within a single nanosec-

III Mind and Time

ond, there is observation, mind sensing an object, and thought identifying it; the instant thought is, meaning is. In the next nanosecond, as the senses grasp at the object, we may pick up a feeling and react: "I don't like this." But without the first nanosecond in which identity and recognition take place, that feeling and the thought that follows it cannot occur.

To generate the nanosecond, mind marks out units based on reflections. In much the same way that mind recognizes objects and establishes them as real, it points out, identifies, labels, and validates nanoseconds with the stamp of recognition. With each validation, mind reflects back to itself. It confirms yes, that is a nanosecond; yes, that is a unit of time.

To see how this works, imagine a dialogue between Mind and Perception:

Mind: I give you space/time.

Perception: How much?

Mind: The nanosecond.

Perception: Thank you. Now I have to act.

[Perception enters and begins to discriminate—'yes' to this, 'no' to that.]

Mind: I have provided this opportunity. I have projected the nanosecond and established time.

Is Mind overstating its role, here? No. For, if mind marks out the nanosecond, and this marking out initiates all the operations that follow, time as we know it is literally made by mind. Moreover, each subsequent operation of mind is implicit in the first nanosecond, for all the conditions are already present. The stage is ready, the script has been written, and each of the actors is ready to play the role that mind has assigned. Everything is prepared, awaiting activation at the instant of recognition. So, when mind pronounces, "I feel bad" or "I am happy" 'feel bad' and 'happy' are absolutely true.

Identity leaves no space for doubt, so it cannot fail. "I feel bad; I am happy." Yes, because these thoughts have been stamped into consciousness by the mechanism of recognition. The process unfolds automatically, because this is the way mind has set up the rules.

Mechanism of Recognition

Projecting the nanosecond, mind also projects the time frame in which cause and effect can occur. It is as if mind takes two roles—mind as mind and mind as time—and collaborates with itself,

III Mind and Time

saying, "I will give myself [as time] the opportunity to create the frame for an object to manifest. As soon as an object appears within it, I will provide the instant that allows me to capture and identify it." Given this instant, identity happens, followed by naming, recognition, associations, interpretations, and dialogues between mind and its retinue. As mind's regime falls into line, the process gathers momentum. All this takes place within the frame created as mind projects the nanosecond. But we have no way to think about it before recognition takes place.

Where did this process begin? What caused it to begin? We can say that mind picks up sensory stimulations and generates thoughts in the process of cognizing, identifying, naming, and recognizing, but until we can trace the operations of mind to their origin, prior to the point of recognition, our knowledge remains incomplete.

A Landing Place for the Mind

The point of recognition—the interval of the nanosecond—provides a kind of 'landing place' for mind, a point of reference for a segment of reality that mind builds upon and returns to for reassurance and validation. We see this process operating whenever we tell ourselves, "I have seen that, I have heard that. I thought it. I remember it. It happened. I believe it; it is true." But remember that, by the time we say "it happened," the first instance of contact with sensory vibrations is long since past. Only the reflections of the image are being recalled, re-cognized, and re-understood: we are far from direct contact with reality. What we have are but glimpses and assumptions, gleaned from reflections in the mirror of mind.

We experience this entire process as instantaneous; or rather, we experience only its results. But if we could slow it down and observe its stages, we would know more clearly how perception works. We would understand the significance of naming, identity, and recognition. We would know how mind makes language, how language characterizes perceptions, and how mind uses language to interpret and comment. We might realize there is little or no opportunity to deliberate the stages of this process or to make informed decisions—all of the ingredients that make up experience already exist. They are prepared and ready to go at any moment, in any and all directions, and to any place. Mind simply

III   Mind and Time

assembles them and presents us with something 'understandable' that we can use and convey to others. This innate readiness to manifest experience instantaneously may be what the word 'existence' implies.

28

Labels and Identity: Building the Master Pattern

For all the phenomena we recognize, for everything picked up by the senses and grasped as an object, mind has a label pre-established and pre-formed, encoded with thoughts, feelings and associated patterns of emotional and physical reactions. Stamped and sealed at the point of recognition, the label serves as proof of identity and a basis for interpretation. In using the label, we automatically affirm that we understand its connotations and associations.

Like a coat that wraps around the body, concealing the specifics of what lies behind, labels conceal the true nature of what we perceive. In wearing a label, mind manifests the identity of that label and carries on its characteristics. Over time, labels take on a sense of reality that we are likely to hold on to for the rest of our lives.

Labels express meaning in a certain way; each has its own features, connotations, and associa-

III Mind and Time

tions, and each of these in turn has its own definition and description. Each description has a certain application, and each application has its set of meanings, all custom-tailored to express the nuances of specific situations, relationships, disciplines, and purposes.

Usage, repetition, and development through the centuries have shaped labels into the building blocks for language and civilization. Identifying, recognizing, naming, thinking and acting, human beings have migrated to all parts of the planet. Hunting, farming, weaving, establishing settlements, defining and playing social roles, they have developed large empires, civilizations, and systems of education, evolving countless languages to accommodate the continual expansion of information and the ever-changing needs of diverse populations.

As beneficiaries of all that has come before, we tend to think that we stand at the highest peak of human development. But we all come from the same basic point, the unit of experience that allows perception to take place. From this unit comes our reality: the regime of mind that establishes subject and object, and with it, the way of seeing that distinguishes self from everything else and creates the conditions for separation.

Labels and Identity

All of us live within the context of family, society, culture, and nation, but at an even more fundamental level, we live in a world of labels and concepts and we express our understanding through language. The rules related to our labels and the patterns of cognition that establish them are the most deeply imprinted of all. They prevent us from even conceiving of a way of thinking that does not depend upon subject and object, the contrasts of pro and con, and the continual pulling 'to' and pushing 'from' that characterize our dualistic orientation. Perception of subject and object is seemingly hard-wired into our being along with patterns of emotionality, desire, feeling-tones, and responses. All of these operate predictably without our conscious direction. All of them flow through mind and thoughts and find expression in our embodiment.

Living out the Pattern

We are bonded to ways of thinking and doing that have changed very little over many thousands of years, and our lives are constricted by the way these systems are set up. We have the master pattern, the rules to maintain the pattern and the roles to enforce it; and the players,

III Mind and Time

ourselves, perfectly conditioned to apply and extend it. Everything is captured, from our environment and living conditions to our ways of participating in our culture and communities. Perceptions, thoughts, feelings, memories, and speech are perfectly integrated into the system, as if designed to support and perpetuate it.

Everyone now plays the game the same way, and each of us reflects it to others. Within this framework, we endure a subtle, yet pervasive kind of bondage, lured on by promises of pleasure and hopes of success, and driven from behind by doubts, worries, dissatisfaction, fear, and the overpowering need to fit in. Captured by the orientation of our minds, we think and act in accordance with the patterns mind has developed. From birth to death, the patterns continue to govern our lives. Unless some radical shift in view adjusts the rules and changes the direction of this orientation, we will follow the model already established until our time on earth comes to an end.

As we enact our roles, we feel compelled to satisfy expectations and desires—our own and those of others. We have obligations. We are busy. We suffer from frustration, mental and physical pain, and discontent, all of which drain the energy of body and mind until our very cells are exhausted. We cannot opt out or refuse. Everyone has to participate, which may help explain why we are so often tired and sick.

The Illusion of Progress

Some might say that we do not have to continue on this way, but we do not know of any other. By naming, defining, and categorizing, collecting data and shaping structures that can be expanded infinitely, we set in motion the processes that now sustain our way of being in the world. Among them are identity and recognition, the back-and-forth of confirmation and validation, positioning of subject and object, observation of cause and effect, operation of the senses, awareness of feeling, discriminations and judgments, and the thoughts, ideas, and memories that comprise our human history and fundamental patterns of response.

At some point we became aware of a director with a decision-making function, an entity named 'mind'. As director, mind created the regime that now governs our thoughts and perceptions and developed language as its tool for

III Mind and Time

anchor in reality, we cling to it tightly, justifying it as part of 'the way things are' or perhaps as divine will, ennobled through atonement or martyrdom. In doing so, we blind ourselves to a major source of needless pain.

Can We Envision a Better Model?

Can we afford to ignore the suffering that this understanding of reality generates? Leaders among us have created impressive buildings, conquered powerful enemies, made millions in the stock market, gained power over many thousands of people, or become known throughout the world. But what do such accomplishments mean after we are no longer alive? Our lives and all our resources may have been dedicated to such activities, as have the lives and resources of countless others, generation after generation repeating the same model, building on what came before. But this way of living and acting has perpetuated the kinds of suffering that we have endured throughout human history. It has also nourished the seeds of separation and disharmony, cultivated from the outset in our patterns of perception and expressed in nearly every aspect of our language and culture.

Labels and Identity

Since these seeds tend to proliferate, we might well wonder whether at some point they will they crowd out our capacities to broaden and deepen our understanding of human being. As we depend ever more strongly on labels and concepts clouded by assumptions, judgments, and self-oriented concerns, at what point will awareness and clarity become sterile concepts rather than fundamental human attributes?

Our present regime of mind may have become unnecessarily confining, a product of an earlier age that the dynamic power of time has rendered obsolete. Since this regime activates automatically once mind projects the nanosecond—the unit of experience that allows perception to take place—a fuller understanding of time might reveal possibilities for a different kind of regime, one able to lead us through the walls of mind and reveal the full beauty of being. To explore further, we need to look more closely at the relationship of mind and time.

29

The Forward Thrust of Time

We experience time as going forward, unfolding in a linear progression. As we move in time the past stretches behind us, becoming ever more distant history, while the future emerges, allowing opportunities for change and new experiences to occur.

Morning gives way to afternoon. When nighttime comes, afternoon becomes the past and morning recedes further, becoming the more distant past. We organize time into units we can measure and manage, characterizing 'this time' and 'that time', morning, noon, and night. Relying on such observations, we mark out the segments of our days and give the name of 'time' to these segments, dividing up through language what we actually experience as continuity. In this culture, at least, it is universally accepted that time moves forward and can be divided into past, present, and future.

The Forward Thrust of Time

Although we do not know the cause for time's apparent movement, we sense the passing of time and note transitions we consider significant. Our minds have endless stories that affirm this is true.

Time in this sense is not an object we can measure—it is the measurement itself, the yardstick devised by mind to identify, situate, and communicate experience, our own and that of humanity from its earliest origins. More accurately, it is the label we give to this measurement, a label that tends to distance us from the meaning of what it represents.

What then, does the label 'time' represent? What does it point to? What is its meaning?

Mind in the Three Times

Every dimension of human experience—including culture, history, religion, faith, philosophy, psychology, and anything our imagination projects—is framed in the context of three dimensions of time (past, present and future) and experience: past memories, present feelings, and future-oriented imaginings that give rise to hope and expectations.

III Mind and Time

Within these three dimensions of time and experience, mind acts in the present. It identifies objects and relates them to the purposes of the subject 'I', much as a customer shops for items to bring home and enjoy. But what mind gives us is a reflection, not the genuine experience— a pale imitation already clothed in assumptions and interpretations. Fixated on the subject-oriented point of view, mind misses points of transition that could lead to a direct involvement with the dynamic unfolding of being.

Without realizing the treasury of potentials that mind has already overlooked or dismissed, we pursue pleasure and satisfaction as best we can, experiencing happiness, pain, well-being, suffering, misery, joy, and more, in no particular order. A shifting array of emotional and psychological states captures and occupies our attention. While mind tracks their rise and fall and responds to events that pop up from moment to moment, the operations of its regime obscure the emerging dynamic we call 'present' time, where all we most value—life, time, freedom, choice, and opportunity—is slipping away.

The Play of Mind in Time

Continually pre-occupied with recognizing, identifying, and interpreting perceptions, memories, and thoughts, mind pursues, points out, and makes meaning out of everything that stimulates it to respond. From instant to instant, it generates a flow of interpretations, dialogues, and pronouncements. It recognizes, identifies, and speculates on the significance of specific characteristics; it pursues comparisons and associations, analyzing and interpreting feelings and emotions. Easily bored, it may entertain itself by commenting on its own imaginings. "Wonderful!" "Miserable!" "Beautiful!" "Horrible!" "Not healthy." "This is living!" "This is helpful." "This is happiness!"

Mind gives itself room to play and replay all manner of roles, going from place to place, reflection to reflection, moment to moment, moving forward towards identity and recognition and back again into uncertainty and doubt. Mind dictates, points out, gives feedback, and identifies and announces continuity. Each pronouncement is another expression of mind, validated by the perceptual processes that mind has established.

III Mind and Time

Cognizing, recognizing, memorizing, and being aware, mind exercises its creative potential, shaping time—and our experience—into past, present, and future. In this way, it provides itself the stage it needs to play its roles and enact its version of reality. In accepting the limitation of the three times that mind sets up, we create the continuum that perpetuates identity—the continuum of our own actions, interacting, bouncing back, bouncing forward, feeding back, filling the clear openness of mind with echoes, re-establishing reality instant by instant.

Bondage of Mind: Mind Out of Touch

If we are honest, we will admit that we are not fully at home in the realm mind has structured. From time to time, we sense that something is missing or is not quite right. If we were really secure in mind's reality-structure, would we experience so much uncertainty? Would so many of our choices lead to frustration and pain? Would we lose touch with meaning and purpose, or be so easily bored or depressed? Too often, we hear the siren of an inner alarm system, saying "I am not happy. This is not fair. I should not have to feel this badly. This has been going on far too long. I don't know what it is, but something is wrong. Isn't there a better way?"

This is the bondage of mind, the mind that forces us into servitude by the nature of its own operations. Ruled by this mind, we are sealed into the illusory reality-realm created by mind's regime, effectively locked out of authentic communication with the deeper currents of our being. Dependent on labels and interpretations assigned by mind, we cannot set aside notions of past, present and future and experience directly what mind presents.

30

A Seeming Continuity

Without the linear framework of time, there could be no causal connection between one event and another. Since it is the function of the cause to produce the effect, common sense and logic place the cause or reason for an event prior to its effect. If there were no past, there would be nothing that could be responsible for an event happening in the present. And if there were no future, the results of present events would have no opportunity to manifest: Cause and effect would be completely separate, with no connection between them. What is moving into the past has to leave the stage of the present, otherwise the future has no place to manifest. But some 'current' continues on, linking the cause that is moving into the past with the future that will manifest the effect. This continuation—what seems to be happening now—is what we call the present. Thus we assume that cause and effect must play out in the context of past, present, and future.

Examining Cause and Effect

The present can be thought of in terms of a constant continuation that is vibrant and dynamic. Rhythm after rhythm, motion after motion, rising and falling like waves on the ocean, the present carries the motion of the cause, enabling effects to appear as the future comes forward to take the present's place. The momentum of the cause brings the effects to us in the present, which was the future when the causal event took place. We could say that the causal event is 'deposited' in the future, to mature, like a seed, in a future present.

Cause and effect do not happen simultaneously, but at different times and at vastly differing intervals. We may not always be able to predict when the effects of a given cause will come: twelve months from now, thirty days, an hour, a minute, a second, or less. But even without knowing this, we accept as factual and real the ordered system that governs causation. Our reasoning reinforces the supposition that there is a causal continuity associated with time; there

III Mind and Time

is movement, and that movement is toward a future that has not yet appeared. At the same time, the rhythms of the present move the continuum toward the past.

The only point where the cause could have a causal connection with the effect is at the exact point when the present is replaced by the past. To serve its purpose of linking cause and effect, this point where the past gives way and the present has not yet come would have to be almost inconceivably small, even smaller than the nanosecond.

Considering Nanoseconds

Imagine that nanoseconds are cylinders made up of slices of past, present, and future. Suppose there are fifteen such segments, each with its own specific character and role to play. Thus, in the past we can distinguish: 1) the very remote past; 2) the not so remote past; 3) the intermediate past; 4) the immediate past; and 5) the immanent past, just before the present arises. For the present, there is 1) the present poised on the verge of receding into the past; 2) the continuing present; 3) the present moment of experiencing (like the first two, already moving toward the past); 4) the present just beginning to manifest,

A Seeming Continuity

freshly coming into view; 5) the still undefined 'cutting edge' of the present, moving to take its place as it emerges from the future. As for the future a similar fivefold progression could be said to operate, 'stocking' the future, but since the future remains unstructured and undefined, it cannot be treated in the same manner as past and present. We can say only that the future supplies the present.

By breaking each nanosecond down in this way, we might seem to be making progress in explaining how cause and effect might operate within the context of past, present, and future. But the procedure is not entirely satisfactory. While each of these fifteen aspects functions in a certain way to connect cause and effect, the nature of the connection itself remains mysterious.

Points of Transition

Of course, there is no law stating how nanoseconds are to be divided. For example, we can halve the intervals again, and then again, moving as close as possible to the point where existence begins, where 'not yet happened' becomes 'happening,' where 'not-exist' becomes 'exist'. Even here there is no reason to stop. We

III Mind and Time

might envision the beginning or transition point as itself an elliptical disk with many billions of points moving very fast along its forward edge. This would be the 'cutting edge' of the present moving to 'take place'.

But perhaps we are missing other possibilities. What if each of the fifteen units of each nanosecond were to move in a random, non-linear way? In that case, do we have any way to say with certainty which point connects with which, or even which unit is cause and which is effect? Can we tell which point provides each character and quality of the present, which provides quantity, or which influences a certain way of behavior?

Here is another possibility: Imagine, instead, the fifteen units within the nanosecond arrayed in a single horizontal line, with other nanoseconds flowing beneath them in their own horizontal array. The fifteen units arrayed along the top are the ones we have assumed carry the momentum of cause and effect from past to future. Yet suppose each of these fifteen units has fifteen additional units extending from it vertically. From each of these additional units extends a third generation of fifteen units, and from these a fourth generation, and so on through fifteen generations.

A Seeming Continuity

Or perhaps our nanosecond-units unfold in a circular way, not only on a plane, but in depth and into all directions. Eventually they would merge and become one like the elliptical disk described above.

Among all these possibilities, there is still no point of transition that goes beyond the fifteenth unit, no 'landing place' where mind can initiate its operations so that the link between cause and effect can be established. Perhaps here, at the edge of beyond, before the next series of units, we could posit a smaller, sixteenth unit, the elusive point of transition. Indivisible, unoccupied, and uncommitted, yet not stagnant or locked in, the point of transition is fluid and open, like a brilliant bubble of quicksilver, a window of opportunity that allows experience to be.

In this realm of the infinitesimally small, points of transition remain mysterious, a kind of non-unit belonging neither to past or future. Time itself might behave in unusual ways, transforming itself into a different reality, possibly governed by different laws. In such a transformed reality, would mind be freed of the minding operations that shape our ordinary ways of being, rendering very different all that we know? If so,

III   Mind and Time

understanding points of transition could mean understanding the illusory nature of what we now view as unchanging and real. It could mean understanding impermanence and the whole context of life and death.

31

Opening the Nanosecond

Working with nanoseconds has the potential to open up the fields of the senses, allowing us to see wider dimensions of space and understand all appearances as projections of mind. Although this understanding will not take us beyond the walls erected by mind's loyalty to a subject/object perspective, opening up our commitment to one single point may make it easier to open others as well.

Can we open up the nanosecond? While words are not likely to be helpful here, we are free to experiment with our own minds. To start, envision the mind as a camera taking photos in rapid-fire succession. Normally, our minds operate much faster than any camera. But if we sit very still in a calm environment without much external sensory stimulation, we may be able to relax our senses enough to slow down the shutter-speed of mind and let the nanosecond become available.

III Mind and Time

Now imagine opening the aperture of mind very wide, a full 360 degrees. You may now be able to glimpse instants when raw sensing begins to take shape and form. You may even be able to pay special attention to the point in this process when mind grasps a form, and feelings, emotions, concepts, and streams of thought begin to arise.

Is this even possible? As you read and re-read these chapters on mind and time, relax and open mind as widely as possible to what is being communicated, and the range of the possible may expand. There will be much that cannot be understood directly through words and meanings. But there are other dimensions that have not yet been explored.

Interlude: Lost in the Nanoseconds

> Here I am, in the present. However I try,
> however diligently I trace out the strings
> of nanoseconds, I am still in the present!
> I do not seem to be crossing over to the future.
>
> It is almost as if someone were scolding:
> "Are you still going back and forth among those
> nanoseconds? How can you expect
> to get to the future if you keep stopping here?
> You have been playing here long enough!
> Quit that!

Opening the Nanosecond

If you are not playing around with
nanoseconds, why are you stalled
in the present? If you have no reason
for staying here, how can there
even be nanoseconds?"

No matter—even if nanoseconds
are not truly real, we can still mark out
units of time and call them nanoseconds.

We cannot argue with nanoseconds.
If we argue with the nanoseconds
we are arguing with time,
we are arguing with reality,
we are arguing with our experience—
we are arguing with our lives.

Alternate Views

The division of time into past, present, and future accommodates the notion of cause and effect, although it leaves the crucial operations of transition and continuity unexplained. But this division is only one way of considering time in relation to mind. Suppose that our conventional notion of time were upended, and we had not just three temporal dimensions to consider, but six, seven, or more. Could time still unfold as a linear continuity, or would everything be in a state of chaos? Possibly everything would collapse, or perhaps

III Mind and Time

nothing we know would have ever existed. For without past, present, and future, there would be no connection between cause and effect: cause and effect could not operate; they could not even exist.

Let's try again. Imagine that we could mark out one given point that represents the center of existence. That point would have to be there in the first nanosecond, because without it, there would be no possibility of a future. There would be no character, no quantity, no physical forms, no realm of things and no things to populate a realm. There would not even be any place that is unoccupied, for there would be no borders. With no borders, there would be no place for cause and effect to manifest; there would be no universe, no existence, not even space.

This imagining is not so far-fetched. In the remote primordial state before the universe and all its forms existed—the past of the past of the past—space was unoccupied and non-existent. This was a kind of first point, a center of all and everything. That once unoccupied point is now our realm of existence, our universe, the entire cosmos with its billions upon billions of stars, planets, and world-systems. How interesting to imagine this transition, from once unoccupied

Opening the Nanosecond

place to the fullness of existence manifesting in infinite variety, characters, and forms! Does this transition depend on cause and effect?

We can go further: consider all forms that have or could possibly exist—all materials and manifestations imaginable and unimaginable, those that have disappeared in the past, those extant in the present, and those that will come into being. Consider them all appearing, exhibiting their unique characters, dancing in time and space, interacting, causing and effecting, producing in different ways manifold realms of existence. For such an array of forms to be established, cause and effect would seem necessary.

Before there was existence, before there was a universe filled with forms, before cause existed as cause, the cause itself had to manifest in a way that enabled it to become the effect. It had to 'take place', in order to bring about an effect. But this would mean there was something 'before' the cause. For, before the cause could arise, there had to be a functioning instrument that could transmit some kind of continuity. Before time, after time, continuation must therefore continue, transmitted by a process we can only call 'continuity'. But the instrument itself, along with its operation, goes unexplained.

32

Ground of Illusion

Before the universe existed, there must have been a 'before', a point, large or small, where the necessary conditions could converge and set in motion the process that allowed the universe to come to be. Mind requires a similar kind of 'before', a point from which its minding business can unfold our own mental universe.

Bridge to Wholeness and Clarity

With each such point—each new 'before', mind spins out a new illusion, like the rapid-fire camera imagined in the last chapter. The reflections of these illusion-images within mind create as well the illusion of movement and continuity. We sense 'time is passing', moving forward. Recognition by recognition, instant by instant, the mechanisms of mind give rise to a new reality based on each new 'before'. Reflecting on this, we might

Ground of Illusion

want to consider more carefully the nature of what came 'before'.

In order to arrive at a point before minding, a point that is clear and unoccupied, enabling experience to develop from a stable foundation, mind needs to calm down its restless jumping from thought to thought. But if this were ever possible in the past, as the pace of change quickens and life grows more chaotic, it becomes increasingly difficult. Catastrophic events, new technology, and major social and cultural changes unfold ever more rapidly, challenging mind to make sense of these changes and to incorporate them into its processes. Instead of calming down, mind is pressured to speed up. The result is that mind tends to communicate with the senses more roughly. Critical aspects of the perceptual process may not link up so smoothly with identity and recognition. Then mind, anxious for resolution, may grasp at incorrect interpretations, distorting the accuracy of thoughts and feelings and increasing the likelihood of misunderstanding.

This intensifying busy-ness of mind separates us even more from the instant before all minding activities, where mind functions in wholeness and clarity. To reach this point—to cross over the

III Mind and Time

ocean of swirling mental activity—we would seem to need some kind of bridge. But we cannot even think about where that bridge might be found if our patterns of identity, labeling, and recognition are pointing us in the wrong direction by instilling a false notion of subject and object, and distorting our understanding of time.

Misunderstanding time, we relate to it wrongly and become caught up in illusions. Since mind and senses fail to alert us to the nature of these illusions, there is no incentive to understand and wake up to other possibilities. We take our point of view and all that follows from it to be incontrovertibly real, based on the observations of our senses and the rational processes of our minds, inhabiting what in some philosophic traditions is known as relative reality.

'Relative', in this sense, could be said to refer to whatever appears real within the scope of thought and concepts of past, present, and future. We know this territory and system from within. We know that it leads to restrictions and problems.

To free ourselves of these restrictions and problems, we need a different operation of mind, one that engages the dynamic of time more intimately. This would bring us face to face with impermanence, the continual falling away of the familiar and the emergence of the new.

Impermanence is the reality in which our lives unfold, a constant reminder of the change and loss that underlies our most persistent forms of suffering. Rather than attempting to dismiss in vain the implications of impermanence, it seems important to continue to investigate further mind's relationship to time, to cross the bridge to the instant before minding, to the clear, uncluttered landscape of mind prior to the instant from which all systems and 'mindings' arise.

Tracking the Beginning and Ending of Thoughts

In the process of perception, the interaction of senses and mind joins the physical and cognitive streams of our being, Sensory stimulation results in identity, labeling, and recognition, and we awaken within the realm of mind, our cognitive and intellectual processes fully operative. We are aware that we exist, that we are here in the present, that we arrived here 'from' some prior experience, and we sense we are going 'toward' some new experience that has not yet arrived.

III Mind and Time

Within this structure, every perception or thought must have a beginning and an end, a 'head' that is pointing toward what is coming up and a 'tail' as the perception or thought gives way, allowing another perception or thought to come up. We find ourselves asking: What was before the identity and recognition that brought us this thought or instant of perception? There must have been a before, but it is unknown. What comes after this perception or thought ends and the next one has not yet been identified and recognized? This 'after' is also unknown.

Mind as we experience it is thus linked to identity. Before identity, we cannot recognize the existence of anything, not even ourselves. So we might also ask, where are we before we exist, before identity has summoned the subject into being and labeling has given it the name of 'I'?

For all we know, the 'before' of our present situation may very well be empty space. When perception happens, our present universe bursts into being, as if it had manifested inside of a gigantic bubble. We assume it is the same universe we experienced an instant before, but one perception had to end before the next could begin, so we cannot know. Each instant of our

Ground of Illusion

conscious, waking life is bounded by a territory that is unknown, a 'before' and 'after' where identity, labeling, and recognition are not operating. The coming into being of our mind-universe is repeated instant by instant, perhaps hundreds or even thousands of times a second, perhaps a thousand times in each nanosecond. What we perceive as continuity may be better understood as a series of discrete perceptions.

Even if we lack all access to the before and after, we can study this process by observing the beginning and end of thoughts. How a thought begins, how a thought finishes, and what lies between the end of one and the beginning of another: these are the places to be aware. This is what we wish to observe more and more closely.

Time goes forward—moving ahead to the not known. The 'from' is not known, the 'to' is also not known. The 'before' of this present situation may have been only empty space.

How to understand? Exercise every head and tail of perception! How much is unknown? How great is the gap between known and known? Look not just once, but every second. How does it occur?

III   Mind and Time

of our ordinary awareness, activated by receptors sensitized through prior experience and conditioning, all kinds of images could bubble up from imagination and dreams and blend into our thought processes, from where they could manifest in unexpected ways.

Reflections in the Mirror of Mind

An image in a mirror may appear three-dimensional, but on closer inspection we see that its dimensionality is only an illusion, created by light reflecting off a flat surface. Similarly, the image of the moon in a pond breaks up when the water is disturbed, revealing that there is nothing there—no moon, not even any image of the moon.

Suppose the images that appear in mind are similar, like holograms or projections. There is no 'basis' for a hologram: it has no 'from'. No one constructed it. It has no physical shape or form, nor any substance that could serve a function in time and space.

The images in mind might be much like this, arising from impressions shimmering on the sensitive, mirror-like surface of mind. Sensing, identity, labeling, re-cognition, interpretation, and imaginings weave narratives that feed back to

Sensitivity of Mind

our eagerly acquisitive customer minds. Reaching back to the past, scraps of narratives awaken memories and associations; moving forward, they unfold with their own sequential logic. Interacting, overlapping, looking back, moving forward, weaving stories that make sense, they convince us that they are real. But however real they appear to be, they may be projections that have no substantial foundation.

Seeds of Suffering

Misunderstanding mind's sensitive, shimmering quality, the regime of mind initiates the process of perception and shapes it toward existence. The 'cause'—identity and recognition—produces the 'effect', our view of what is. Now mind is ready for confusion and all manner of emotional obscurations. We do not have a choice in the matter: once the regime of mind engages sensory impulses in its characteristic mistaken way, we cannot choose not to suffer.

Perceptions seem to arise spontaneously and instantaneously, in a nanosecond or less. Each nanosecond in turn, occupied by images and energized by mind, engages the established patterns of perception that conduct mental energy

III Mind and Time

into the programs set up by mind. Attachment arises along with grasping and polarity, the recognition of subject and object that sets up mind's dualistic orientation. All this happens whether the perception is painful or routine, or whether it happens in prayer, meditation, or visualization.

These processes are both incredibly fast and firmly interlocked. The senses grasp, initiating cognition; mind identifies, labels, and validates through recognition, stimulating thoughts, interpretations, meanings, characteristics, and discriminations, with emotions following close behind, like infantry divisions on the march. The heavy artillery follows, carrying an array of powerful weapons: desire, attachment, anger, ignorance, and more. In a flash this army has taken command of the field of our experience.

If it were possible to reduce the speed of our perceptual process, the first instance of recognition might be less likely to engage the regime of mind that propels us into confusion and emotional turmoil. This is why meditation, prayer, and contemplative exercises may provide some measure of relief. By neutralizing and stabilizing the ordinary activity of mind, calming practices slow the speed of sensory impulses, lessening their impact and diminishing the sense of time passing. But as long as the operations of mind unfold in a linear fashion, from one instant to the next, they will not enable us to transcend the temporal order of past, present and future established by mind. Our frame of reference will still be the illusory realm of cause and effect created by mind's regime. Within this frame, we can arrive at truth, but whatever truth we experience will be limited.

34

The Engine of Mind

We have been investigating how units of mind-perception—identity, name and meaning, sealed and validated by recognition—form unique chains of mental events that become the basis for our sense of what is true and real. We have seen how mind views this reality in a way that polarizes perception into a dualistic mode that gives rise to subject and object, self and other. Recognition engages the chain of cause and effect, and the momentum that results drives the programs of mind.

Some philosophies use the concept of cause and effect to explain the automatic and relentless way that mind's patterns continue, growing more complex over time. The more complex the patterns, the more variety we perceive, convincing us that something 'new' is happening. So we keep going on, hoping for something that will awaken more interest and meaning in life, hop-

The Engine of Mind

ing that things will improve, hoping that tomorrow will somehow be different than today.

Since our observations confirm that there is indeed change, our hopes continue. But the patterns governing experience go on as before. The endless cycles of cause and effect they create lead us through varied landscapes of mind that range from ecstasy and bliss to extremes of loneliness and confusion. Yet, behind all this movement is a sense of dullness and disconnection, a product of the essentially repetitious and aimless activity that characterizes much of our lives.

The engine driving these patterns is the process of perception, and perception in turn seems driven by a certain kind of anxiety. The senses are alert, actively searching for something to perceive, while mind is poised in readiness to identify and recognize what the senses present. There is an underlying tension, experienced as a deep, subliminal urge: "Have to get there; must have it." As the urge grows stronger, we become more aware of the subject: we have to get somewhere, we have to have something.

Perception pushes for identity and recognition, which resolve uncertainty and allow mind an instant to relax. But even this limited resolution

III   Mind and Time

does not always progress smoothly. When the push toward 'have to get' is blocked by 'cannot get', internal pressures tend to activate patterns of agitation and frustration.

Conflicting Currents of Dualistic Mind

Committed to a dualistic orientation, mind manifests in ways that can be contradictory and confusing. Sometimes mind displays the persona of a sympathetic friend or a practical business person; another moment it may turn on us, undermining our self-confidence and filling us with apprehension and fear. Depending on the conditions and circumstances at work, mind and its regime can call forth an array of emotions and attitudes, from lonely and despairing to rich, healthy, and joyful. One moment we may feel confident and in control. On the downswing, the story is very different. As soon as we get settled in one place, mind moves to another, then another, and yet another.

Wanting and not wanting, wishing and dreading, waiting and hoping, always needing more—the shadows of this dualistic mind keep rising up and we simply live with them. So boring, so repetitive, yet also so magnetizing! For some, this back and forth, up and down rhythm brings a

The Engine of Mind

sense of drama into ordinary routines that cuts through boredom and makes them feel engaged and alive.

It is not surprising that fictions based on this familiar rhythm are nearly guaranteed to hold our interest. Reading a novel or watching a film, we can experience strong emotions without exposing ourselves to the consequences of events because we know that in fact the words or images we are encountering are not 'real'.

We could experiment with viewing mind's programs in the same way. If we knew that we could change the focus of our minds as easily as we can turn the page of a book or change a television channel, how might that understanding transform the 'locked-in' quality of our lives?

Understanding mind without being locked in to its regime, we would see more clearly the patterns that drive the ups and downs of our lives: the blissful happy times, the anxious and devastating times, and the lost and hopeless times. We would understand that the convoluted coding in the programs run by mind's regime developed in response to conditions that may no longer apply to us today. This understanding would free us of the impulse to respond automatically and give

III   Mind and Time

us pause to take a more appropriate direction. Aware of the futility of replaying or justifying each twist and turn of our stories, we might find ways to develop a more original approach to our own lives, based on a mind free of confining walls and fixed positions. Processed differently, less constricted by past emotions and stale expectations, experience might reveal more purely the beauty and dynamic power of mind itself.

35

Another Kind of Mind

We can imagine that, prior to perception, mind is a radiant arc open 360 degrees in all directions, and suffused with laser-like beams of light. If we could enter such a prior dimension, we would see a world not yet shaped by the operation of cause and conditions. In this pristine realm, the view from wherever we stood would be the same. Surrounded by light rays moving rapidly and randomly, it would be hard for us to distinguish a center, an end, or a beginning. We might even have to let go of the notions of center, end, and beginning—even the notion of a 'present'. Yet in this brilliantly luminous realm, labels, associations, and expectations would fall away, revealing different qualities than we have experienced up to now—qualities that mind has never learned or been taught, has never been exposed to in any way. Experience unfolding within this unbounded vista of mind might find

III   Mind and Time

stand how not to play games and how not to hold on to roles.

From within such understanding, we may now be clear on how mind uses language, how mind points out, how mind interprets, how mind constructs meaning, how mind structures what we view as reality, how mind names and philosophizes about existence and truth, and more. Seeing this, we may be ready to recognize that the human mind does not have to be based on the ordering of concepts, an order that leads us into a no-choice regime.

As long as mind is bound to its present orientation, our intellect will keep playing games, but now we may understand that it is possible to explore mind from a different point of view. Attentive to the processes that drive our responses, we can understand the proud, game-player mind, the creative, imaginative story-teller mind, the behavior-carrier mind, the knowledge-holder mind, and the mind that gives us language, interpretations, and meaning. The more we understand, the more options we have and the more informed will be our choices. The options presented by understanding will be ever freer from the delusions constructed for us by our ever-creative role-playing mind.

Another Kind of Mind

This understanding works for everyone: no special knowledge or skills are required. It shows us that mind is flexible, that our way of being is not cast in concrete. We do not have to be great thinkers, or spiritually oriented, or practitioners of meditation to open up alternatives and take advantage of them.

So open your mind wide to possibilities and allow yourself to engage them. Let the processes of minding and mind-dialogue begin. Let it uncover and feed back alternatives. Think about knowing, think about mind's way of interpreting, look at the programming that comes between 'I' and mind, leaving us no opportunity to know who we really are. Ask how to connect with mind at the outset, when all is still open and luminous.

Section Four

Ground of Understanding

Looking with fresh eyes at the regime of mind, we begin to see how much we do not understand. But this 'not understanding' is not a signal to give up: it is an invitation to continue. 'Not understanding' is the necessary first step toward understanding—a step that at once acknowledges where mind is now and reveals fruitful areas for further exploration. When we take this step, even a glimpse of understanding can bring more light into mind and enable us to see what we have previously overlooked. Relying on understanding, we have a valuable opportunity to transform our way of being on a very fundamental level.

36

Programmed Dynamic of Mind

Mind captures everything we perceive. It tells us the names of all we know, and it does not make mistakes. Whenever mind perceives an object, recognition is instantaneous: mind taps into programs of response and activates them automatically. Everything necessary to sustain this system appears to be already established, like codes in a computer, fully potentialized in the realm of mind. The operating system is already in place, the basic programs are pre-installed, and the system will now accept only programs that are compatible.

Consider the operations that are now working under various names: awareness, perception, consciousness, senses, feeling, various intensities of frustration and anger, behaviors and feelings related to positive and toxic emotions, and more. Consider also memory, plans and anticipations, images, fantasies, worries, preoccupations, wants, and desires. Their patterns unfold predict-

Programmed Dynamic of Mind

ably from the point of recognition, re-establishing our reality from instant to instant. Like dreams, such patterns may have no real substance or logic. Yet mind continues to refine and expand them in response to internal and external feedback.

If we could disengage from these programs and step back, we might recognize mind's playbook at work: Keep them busy, give them pleasure, give them fun, give them some control. Society works the same way, motivating and educating us by feeding desires, telling us to enjoy, making us more and more busy, involving us in obligations backed by the force of consensus and tradition, wrapping us so tightly in its demands that we can scarcely take a breath. By now these patterns are nearly universal.

No one knows whom to blame. We think, "This is my own choice, this is my own mind, this is the way I am." We are going along with mind, intensifying its momentum, involving ourselves more and more deeply and setting ourselves up ever more surely for disillusion and despair. Unable to conceive of any other way to be, we can only continue down this track, working ourselves further into this system with all that we think and do, fascinated by the flow of events and the emer-

IV Ground of Understanding

gence of new forms. Within this system, change tends to foster instability, confusion and uncertainty—states of mind that bind us even more closely to the way things are.

Mind Divided

Committed to a dualistic orientation, mind manifests in ways that can be contradictory and confusing. Depending on conditions and circumstances, mind and its retinue can call forth an array of emotions and attitudes, from fiery, weak, and despairing to rich, healthy, happy, and joyful. As soon as we get settled in one place, mind moves to another, then another and yet another.

As we well know, mind divided against itself can manifest tremendous longing, desire, and frustration. We can cry silently a long time, unable to have something we deeply yearn for. When yearning has no result, mind pushes more strongly for resolution: "I want this, I need that, I'm not getting what I need, I'm not going where I want to go." Pressure increases—first a little agitation, then more intense, spilling into anxiety that grips our whole being. Mind thrashes in frustration and ties itself into knots; flames come

Programmed Dynamic of Mind

up with tremendous force. "Hurry, hurry." "Must have, must do, must have now!"

But we cannot just take what we want. Even if the opportunity presents itself, there are others around us and we need to monitor our actions. Conflicted by hopes and uncertainty and our innate sense of right and wrong, we are likely to restrain or deny our feelings. Frustration is increasing, yet we need to appear in control. Surrounded, blocked on all sides, we may realize how completely we are at the mercy of our own minds.

Wanting, wishing, waiting, and hoping; grasping, driven by desire, torn between the expectation of getting something and anxiety that this might not happen, always needing more, mind can reach the point where it says "I can't stand it!" It wants to hold on, but it cannot; unsatisfied, completely lost, it can become frozen in frustration and self-condemnation.

Pro and con, "have to have," "cannot have"— the shadows of this dualistic mind still flock together, and it seems we have to live with them. There is always a different discussion, a different time, new things, and a new customer. Wild swings of feeling can exhilarate and cast down unpredictably. While we may compare our situation to riding a blind wild horse and realize the

IV Ground of Understanding

potential for serious pain, this back and forth, up and down rhythm seems to be what we want for our experience. Nothing else seems interesting,

Understanding mind, we would understand the programs that drive the ups and downs of our lives. We would understand the convoluted coding in the programs run by all aspects of mind's regime, developed in response to conditions that may no longer apply to us today. Aware of the futility of adjusting each twist and turn or adding more layers to programs already overburdened, we might develop a more original approach based on a broader field of mind, one that is free of walls and fixed positions and served by a different regime. If we input differently, a new version could come out, supported by operations that transmit more purely the beauty and dynamic power of mind itself.

Restructuring the Pattern: First Steps

Once we understand how mind fabricates and dictates, we can explore how we might experience a more satisfying outcome. If we practice observing how the senses and mind work, noting what interactions produce the blissful, happy times we wish to enjoy and which generate anxiety and frustration instead, we will learn to recognize the early stages of toxic emotions and release them before they take hold. Knowing how mind's compounding process unfolds, we could re-direct the mind headed toward depression and release its fixation on thoughts that are making us miserable. Our attitudes and enjoyment of life would improve, and our actions would be more likely to benefit ourselves and others.

Just as a skilled artist can portray all manner of expressions, mind is equally skilled at creating beauty and devastation, as well as all the shades and tones in between. With greater understanding, we can defuse the hair-trigger reactivity that propels our minds into unhappy states and direct mind's brilliance into patterns more likely to produce happiness and peace. As if creating a work of art, we can make our minds so beautiful that they fill our hearts with appreciation and love.

It is our responsibility as human beings to take good care of this mind, to respect its capacities and direct them in ways that do no harm to self or others. If there are secret areas in our psyche that we have kept hidden even from ourselves, it may now be possible to open them up and release deeply held tension and fear. Doing

IV Ground of Understanding

this could inspire confidence to take the next steps. Seeing our results, others might benefit from our example and be encouraged to move in a new direction.

Our duty is not to beat ourselves up with our shortcomings, but to understand how mind works, how it inputs and reads out, and how we can improve the quality of the programs it has mastered so well. However deeply we are involved in our daily lives, we can examine our experience and consider how we may be contributing to our difficulties. In doing so, we begin to ease the conflicting currents of our minds and glimpse possibilities for a lighter, more stable, less burdensome way of being.

37

The Knowing Mind

We have seen how, activated in the process of cognition, mind's regime takes over our mental landscape, dividing it into functions that interact with each other to identify objects and endow them with characteristics and meaning. This activity shapes our orientation to ourselves and the world around us. The instant mind identifies an object, it reflexively creates its polar opposite, and the 'subject' comes into being. The need to name this subject gives rise to the notion of 'I', the coordinator and director, the self that makes distinctions between 'myself' and other.

From one perspective, this subject-object dichotomy is an illusion that arises in the course of perception. But from another perspective, if subject and object were not established, it would not be possible for mind to act. Just as it takes a source of sound and a wall for an echo to be produced, there must be a receiver or knower to pick up the input, or mind could not re-cognize or

IV Ground of Understanding

interpret that input. If mind's knowing and interpretation functions could not interact with one another, the dialogue process that mind depends upon could not develop.

Mind's regime operates constantly, with no delay or gap between one part of the process and another. It activates instantly and automatically like rapid-response radar, pointing out, identifying, labeling, and re-cognizing. Then mind reads out what has just been stamped with the seal of reality. As minding gains momentum, we have thoughts, feelings, images, and forms, each with its specific functions.

While we describe perception as a linear progression, this activity does not seem to have a clear beginning or an end. Mind has a way of cycling round and round, re-interpreting, re-commenting, and re-labeling perceptions it has already named and characterized. It receives, interprets, and understands, then it feeds back the same process again and goes on to more cycles of interpretation.

Repeating, feeding back, and recording continuously within mind, each cycle of mind-activity may produce different thoughts, feelings, and images. Taking the role of an interpreter or intimate friend, mind may patiently explain the meaning of words and perceptions as if it were standing close behind us. It can also shift its role and point of view: having interpreted what we mean, it can organize and broadcast it like an anchorman on the evening news.

After the initial interpretation, a secondary regime takes over, translating the interpretations, selecting what we are looking for, pointing out qualities and characteristics, calling forth memories and associations, revising and re-interpreting all that has gone before. As interpretations become more complex, conflicts can arise, introducing confusion.

Cycles of feedback, re-cognition, re-labeling, and re-interpretation tend to continue. Each time they manifest in a slightly different way, tying up our energy and keeping us off balance and preoccupied. Finally, tired and emotional, uninterested and full of complaints, we may see very little that is positive happening in our lives.

Following the Footprints of Mind

Although we are all familiar with these tracks laid down by mind, it is difficult to follow the footprints of mind to a deeper level. The concepts and

IV Ground of Understanding

dialogues of our ordinary speech do not seem to apply on the deeper levels of mind, where there is knowing, but no knower and no known.

How does the knower know itself? How does the knower know knowing itself? How does knowing acquire the knowledge it knows? We know the knower knows, but we do not know *how* it knows. Using our ordinary language, language custom-designed for us by mind, we can only interpret the nature of mind from a dualistic perspective. Are our interpretations based on arbitrary assumptions? Does mind itself have a history related to cause and effect? At this point, we cannot say.

If there were deeper aspects of mind where the structure of subject and object did not hold, language would have no way to describe it. The only way for mind to connect to or perceive this depth would be within its subject/object perspective. But if deeper levels of mind have in fact nothing to do with concepts of cause and effect, or with emotional obscuration, confusion, greed, hatred, or sin, we will need much more subtle tools than language now provides to understand and explain how mind operates.

As far as we know, we cannot go beyond this realm of mind. Even profound silence or a sense

The Knowing Mind

of inchoate luminosity may be just another among the innumerable ways that mind expresses itself. Mind itself may have a kind of 'minding' quality, and may be capable of great flexibility and manifold ways of expression.

This does not mean that there is nothing about mind we can relate to as real. If mind is not real, we have needlessly built it up into something important. But mind is an intimate part of all our activities, so deeply intertwined with the senses that we cannot refuse to acknowledge it. We cannot deny or ignore it. Yet mind is difficult to capture, difficult to point out, and especially difficult to express through language.

38

Re-Visioning Time and Mind

We would like to contact the interpreter directly, to see the hand reaching out to label forms and thoughts. We would also like to see the back side of knowing, where the 'I' inserts itself. We would like to know where reasoning comes up to determine the right way to judge and evaluate, and we would like to know how cause gives rise to effect. But when we question the 'from' and the 'to' of mind's operations, it becomes difficult to offer explanations, because our questions come from mind, and mind may not be able to connect with itself in this way.

We have already explored a good starting point for a different kind of inquiry: a closer look at how mind interacts with time. Mind measures and marks up time, then points out and interprets, telling us: this point means past; that point means future. But while mind uses time in this linear way to recognize and process experience, this is not the way time actually works. Instead

Re-Visioning Time and Mind

of tracking time from moment to moment, it may be possible to go above and beneath this linear progression and operate from an entirely different perspective.

At present, we have no choice but to address our problems one by one, in the way that mind bound to a linear perspective presents them to us. Such a mind cannot penetrate to the root of our problems, so it is difficult to comprehend how our problems may be related. Yet we know how they tend to manifest in our experience: No sooner is one problem resolved than another comes up in its place. When they come up faster than we can resolve them, we feel overwhelmed.

A more accurate understanding of mind's dynamic—open 360 degrees in all directions—would reveal the threads that connect all of our problems and enable us to cut through them all at once. Tracing the process of pointing out, identity, labeling, recognition, and minding, we may see how mind imposes a linear progression on time, flattening the fullness of its 360-degree perspective into past, present, and future—the province of the intellectual, concept-bound mind.

While we may not yet comprehend the full significance of this operation of mind, we may be

39

Make Room for Understanding

The business that goes on in our mental realm has a dynamic similar to a stock market, with cycles of ups and downs, confidence and confusion, winners and losers, exhilaration and dismay, comfort and discomfort, right and wrong. But we still have no mechanism for investigating how it works, who is overseeing it, who is reporting to whom, where the audience or customers are, who distributed it, how it was manufactured, or who received it. We might even wonder if we can say for certainty that there is a 'who'.

Behind the screened-off area of our inner realm of mind, we may sense a powerful ruler at play. To find out what this entity is doing, we need to go behind the screen. But when we get close to the concealed core of mind, our language becomes too clumsy to take us where we want to go. Our questions do not fit in well with the model and networks set up by mind's regime. Mind's agents—senses, perceptions, cognition,

Make Room for Understanding

identity, and recognition—are busy at work, and all the positions are already filled. There is no opening available for an independent contractor.

Constraints and Constrictions

It appears that the regime of mind has taken over every aspect of our mental processes. The way it operates may be a mystery, but it controls language, mind's medium of communication, and we follow it. We have no words to conceive of or express an alternative. Even our concept of freedom does not seem broad enough to embrace the possibility that we could be free from the regime's all-pervasive control.

Seeing how readily mind slips into this constricted mode of operating, we might wonder if mind might function better with a dual operating system. Perhaps such a system would feature a way of minding less encumbered with an outworn regime and more open to innovations that would provide more liberating options. Possibly this inscrutable magician-mind could access both kinds of operating systems at will, either alternatively or simultaneously.

It may be that such a dual operating system is already at work. Perhaps, at the point of identity

IV Ground of Understanding

and re-cognition, our magician-mind performs a sleight of hand that switches us into our present operating system rather than another. It is possible that we can trace this 'trick' of mind to the process of cognition itself as it unfolds in measured-out time, which is itself a creation of mind.

'Measured-out time' refers to our understanding of past, present, and future. This understanding also may be a fabrication of mind, created to provide a context for reifying our experience. Taking our experience as a baseline, mind may have marked it up in ways that our senses find "reasonable." Mind then validates the senses and interprets its own fabrication through observation: "Witness the sun, witness the seasons, witness your age, witness the changes in your body, witness birth and death." Now you can see: "Yes, there is change. Yes, there is before and after: that which is past, that which is present, and that which is yet to come. Yes, there is time."

In this movement, 'there' indicates the pointing out and 'is' establishes. The label has now been applied, the identity of mind's creation has been sealed and validated. Time now is. The sound of the name has merged with meaning—mind now knows what time is and can apply the

Make Room for Understanding

meaning assigned to that name. From that point of recognition, rooted in the threefold division of past, present, and future, mind relates all our reality, our experience, and our knowledge to the place it has assigned it in time and space.

Reality or Illusion?

Mind presents us with reality as the end product of cognition and links that process to a threefold linear concept of time. But everything depends on how we view the present. If we do not know the starting point, if we cannot stand on the present, we cannot trust that anything we know is real. We need to go further and question what this 'true present' might be.

We ordinarily assume that we know the starting point, that what we experience, think, and do is in present time. But mind, the consummate magician, is very capable of convincing us that our assumptions are real, just as people can make up convincing stories that have no factual basis.

For example, if a new, perhaps unconventional idea pops up suddenly in mind, we might ask ourselves, "Where did that odd notion come from? How could I have thought such a thing?"

IV Ground of Understanding

The next moment, the same idea seems reasonable. Why? Because mind agreed with it. But if you observe carefully, you may note that mind agrees with just about anything. How can we be certain that the 'reality' mind presents to us is truly real?

Amidst the astounding array of roles that it plays, mind continues to manage its recognition time, character-expression time, and pointing-out time. All expressions are allowed, vibrantly interactive in a kind of free-for-all. Top to bottom, sideways, bottom to top, diagonally, or round about—we may not know in which direction mind is moving, but it is very quick and very convincing. Our ordinary intellectual functions cannot keep up with it.

If everything we think and observe is dancing around in the foreground of mind, and minding is going on continuously in the background, then everything is mind, and mind is everywhere; there is nothing apart from mind, nothing it does not encompass, nothing in our experience that it does not condition. Since mind never stops, we will continue to experience the consequences of the illusions it produces. Recognizing this, we move closer to understanding.

Poverty of Knowledge

For many thousands of years, human activity has been adding to the complexity that accumulates in mind: more and more concepts, patterns, interpretations, and models for thought and action. Seeing this vast accumulation, one response is to marvel at how greatly our knowledge has increased. Yet the more concepts and interpretations we come up with, the fewer solutions we seem to have for fundamental human problems. Since we are still using the same operating system of identity and recognition, our proofs for reality are subject to the same basic systems that have been functioning through millennia of evolution.

We need to know more, but we also need a different approach. Most of what we know are assumptions, and assumptions are a major obstacle when we seek to think in unfamiliar ways. Subtly, yet effectively, assumptions allow mind to slip back into familiar patterns, frustrating our efforts to go beyond them.

When we begin to penetrate the fog that assumptions cast on mind, we may meet with strong resistance from mind's regime, which is dedicated to maintaining its routines. And if our

IV Ground of Understanding

interpretations and expressions are not in accord with what others view as logical and right from their point of view, our insights may be invalidated and dismissed. Within and without, we are pressured to go along. Then ego comes in, telling us that we have to act as though we know. Even if we do not understand, we are strongly urged to validate the program: "Yes, I understand, that is right." According to reality. According to mind.

Based on assumptions, we have answers available all the time, but our answers come up within the games we play. As the games progress, they twist and turn, evolving new complexities as they wind through familiar patterns of identity, naming, and recognition. But at some point we may realize that, however creative they may appear, our answers are not providing the solutions expected.

Where to Pay Attention

The more we know about the power of mind, the more helpless we may feel to change our situation. Giving up, saying that there is no answer, there is nothing we can do, is not the point. When such thoughts come up, we can turn them to our advantage and take responsibility for understand-

Make Room for Understanding

ing. A little earlier, we did not have that understanding, but now we may understand that we do not understand. Seeing this brings a measure of relief: Now that we see clearly what we may have been sensing for some time, we can appreciate our insight into the hopelessness of it all.

It can be difficult to accept how thoroughly we are constrained, not by others, but by the mechanisms of our own minds. But with practice, it is possible to gain a sense of how the regime of mind operates, how it alters communications from mind and senses and manipulates thoughts and emotions. If we persevere, we will see this more clearly. As we proceed, we can be guided by our own lack of understanding, knowing that it is pointing out where we need to pay attention. The recognition of not-understanding is the opening to understanding.

40

Turning to Understanding

In the course of functioning in complex societies, everyone learns how to play various roles that he or she may adopt knowingly or unknowingly, as acceptable ways to adjust to our social and working environment. But what effect do these roles have on our views, thoughts, and emotions, which may not fit in quite so smoothly? Mind has its own ways to respond to tensions in our inner environment. It knows the gestures, attitudes, and language that go with specific moods and emotions, and it needs no special education to express them.

Whatever comes up—frustration, confusion, love, aggression, joy, rage, jealousy, or other habitual responses—mind accommodates and expands. Directed by mind, we tend to embody these inner roles as automatically as we adjust to changes in external circumstances. If passion is there, we have to deal with it in some way. If frustration comes up, we may feel an irresistible urge to express it. If anger is driving us, it is possible that we may have already acted it out in ways we will later regret.

Gateway to Understanding

The immediate pull of habitual reactions is so intense that we often do not notice the pattern until it has already occurred. While we may be filled with remorse, punishing ourselves with regret and guilt may only add another layer of response that enables the pattern to continue.

To gain more control over how a situation develops, we need to look more closely at the origins of the pattern. What gave rise to this pattern of response that can take us over and betray our understanding of who and what we are? Who set up the framework that underlies experience? Can we look below the framework to understand who is creating this role and demanding that we play it out in such specific ways?

In the past, with no knowledge of what occurs prior to the reality that mind presents, we would have to accept that reality and respond according to the role mind directs us to play. Now, as we begin to be aware of the pervasiveness of the

IV Ground of Understanding

regime of mind, we have the opportunity to turn this situation around and free ourselves from mind's manipulation.

We can confront mind directly and challenge the ease with which it slips into negative modes of expression. We can question, "Who is telling me that I have to play these games? Who is responding to this demand? Is this role necessary? I no longer wish to participate in this drama." Questioning mind and refusing to own the responses it is urging us to manifest can almost magically lessen the force of strong emotions.

While it may seem impossible at this point to engage time in a way that would transform ingrained patterns of perception and response, we can still question the powerful processes that construct our reality and limit our ability to experience new possibilities for thought and action. Even a few steps in this direction can reveal a gateway to new ways of understanding,

While our situation now is completely locked-in, supported by language and logic, understanding may work in subtle ways that do not rely upon the logical structures of conceptual thought. Perhaps, through our senses, imagination, feelings, or thoughts, we have already picked up enough understanding to appreciate the value of questioning some fundamental assumptions. If so, it will become easier to identify what we do not yet understand and invite understanding to arise.

Even a glimpse of understanding can bring more light into mind and allow us to see what we had previously overlooked. Relying on understanding, we may have the chance to transform our way of being on a very fundamental level.

Benefit of Understanding

Understanding that we have opportunities to reshape our views and perspective is the most precious of gifts. Knowing that we can operate our lives with real choice, that we can exercise mastery without having to BE the master, we find that patterns associated with the need to assert control begin to drop away. With confidence grounded in genuine understanding of our own being, we can say, "I no longer wish to repeat patterns that restrict what I can do and think. I am interested in something more meaningful."

The best agenda is to understand fully, so our choices are based on the best knowledge we can awaken and our actions have meaning and value to ourselves and to others. Like the sci-

IV Ground of Understanding

entific method, but focused on the whole of our being, understanding leads us to research independently and examine the entire context of our lives. It leads us to the true 'fact of the matter'.

Recognizing Understanding

Ultimately, everything is open—all options are available. But to gain access to possibilities that lie beyond its limited frame of reality, mind has to recognize them. Recognition that extends beyond the walls of our dualistic minds comes about through understanding—understanding the processes of mind, understanding that these processes can operate differently, and understanding that through these same processes, mind can free itself from problems and unfold new dimensions of understanding.

For example, when we understand how mind identifies, associates, and interprets, we can say, "I am happy," confident that mind will pick up this thought and develop it. Ordinarily, mind does not sustain such a thought long enough for its benefits to become noticeable or for new patterns to develop. But the greater our understanding and the stronger our aspirations, the more clearly our wishes will imprint on mind, and the more powerfully mind will carry them forward. In the same way, when we understand how mind operates, we can find a way to move past obstacles and be uplifted by all possibilities. When we seek understanding, answers will come.

Redirecting the Dynamic of Mind

Understanding provides leverage, allowing us to re-engineer the mechanisms of minding in ways that bring alive the content and quality of experience. As perceptions are identified, labeled, and affirmed through recognition, as they take form and cycle through associations and interpretations, understanding can engage the dynamic of mind and direct it in more liberating ways.

Understanding works quietly, so it can be difficult to conceive that it could influence mind so strongly. But behind the superficial stream of images that make up our stories, one picture after another, a complex process of design and engineering is at work. When we let understanding take us to this level, we may find that mind operates very differently than we may have expected.

Mind has its own system and its own language, which it uses to input, impose, and interpret in different ways. Human beings have long

IV Ground of Understanding

knowledge relieves the burden of insecurity, confusion, and need, and awakens confidence that requires no external supports. The lighter the burden of self-centered needs, the less dark our problems, and the less pressure afflicts us. Released from hindrances, mind becomes clear, completely open and free.

Foundation for Misunderstanding

Although the natural brilliance of mind has no foreground or background or any other sense of place, mind has to have a point of reference in order to receive and interpret meaning from the flow of sensory impressions. Mind's way of accommodating this need has led to our dualistic way of understanding. Identifying through polarity and contrast, we focus on measurements from here to there and we make distinctions using the language of our customer minds.

As the scope of experience expands, we add more specifics: concepts, private thoughts, memories, and personal habit patterns. Noting differences and relating to them as substantively real, we divide them into categories, assign them territories, erect walls to separate them, and place them in boxes carefully constructed within the

Fooundation for a New Way of Being

walls. While we tend to trust 'our' experience, it is important to realize that we receive every moment of experience according to the way mind presents and interprets it.

As our study of understanding goes deeper, we may question how our divided experience of walls, compartments and zones came to be. Perhaps it is the senses, thoughts themselves, and habitual patterning that together create different categories. Or it could be that language has evolved this way. Possibly mind establishes categories as it scans our experience, isolating what seems relevant and shaping it into reality. If mind's way of operating has limitations, all knowledge that depends on this mind will be limited. Unless we can find ways to operate mind differently, we will continue to receive knowledge according to the structures mind creates to accommodate it.

Using the knowledge that accumulates incrementally through applications of intellect and reason, we have created an ordered way of life that gives us a sense of truth and rightness. Everything has a place and a way of functioning that we can relate to as normal and real. This ensures that our lives will not become

IV Ground of Understanding

disordered and chaotic; it also protects our minds from becoming obsessive, crazed with confusion, or vulnerable to breakdowns.

Having followed these patterns throughout human history, do we have fewer problems and more choices than people who lived in earlier times? Our answers may vary depending on our personal situations and outlook, but when we reflect more globally, most of us are well aware that problems continue to affect the most fundamental necessities of our existence, from the air we breathe to the land that produces our food, from the oceans to the forests and rivers, and from the polar regions to the equator. Since we are still looking for solutions and improvements, trying every day and in every situation to find better ways of being and doing, we seem to be aware that we have something more to understand.

42

Recognizing Misunderstanding

Individually and collectively, we have a duty to ourselves and our societies to recognize the misunderstandings that have slowed our progress and to acknowledge the extent of our not-knowing. But how can we grasp the enormity of what has not yet been understood?

The increasing weight of dissatisfaction, frustration, and agitation that oppresses our minds suggests that something is fundamentally amiss. Internally and externally, problems for which we have no clear solutions threaten to spin out of control. Not knowing, we act: Then consequences come, and we react. But we do not know what came before our action, when we were in a state of not-knowing. We only know the present, right now, when we are already committed to the reaction.

Even in the present, we do not know how troubling thoughts and feelings pop up sponta-

IV Ground of Understanding

neously, often without causes or reasons that we can identify. When we look closely, we sense that something must have prompted them. But if we try to trace them back, mind has gone in another direction, and we cannot connect with the place where these thoughts took birth. Not knowing what gave rise to them, we are left to cope with whatever uneasy feelings follow in their wake.

Tracing the 'prior' of any mental event presents difficulties. Whatever issue comes up, mind may go to several different places at the same time; it may tell conflicting stories and present different alternatives, each convincing in its own way. Confused by mixed messages, we may not know which story to believe, what to choose, or which way to go. Day after day, mind may agitate us this way.

Feelings, thoughts, identity, re-cognition, and associations—mind's whole regime rises up to transport us instantly into different realms of feeling. During the night, when the body sleeps for six to eight hours, mind has free play. We never know where mind might take us, or even if we will awaken in the morning.

If we do not understand how thoughts and feelings come up, we can only accept them as real

Recognizing Misunderstanding

and act on them accordingly. If troubled individuals dwell on thoughts of suicide, mind will help them find a way. Others, who seem more naturally receptive to happy, creative thoughts, will experience a different outcome, but both results are manifestations of mind. Since mind leads and directs, and spirit and body follow, it is important to understand where mind is taking us. How is it that we seek satisfaction and good feelings, yet find ourselves in painful situations? While there are philosophies and theories that address these questions, they all come to us through mind.

Must we accept that we do not know the full context of the thoughts we think or the decisions we make, or fully understand how we came to embrace the ideals and beliefs that are now part of our self-identity? To do so is devastating, which may be why we are in so much denial. When questioned, nearly everyone would say, "That is not true. I know what I am doing, and why. This is the way I think, this is what I believe."

But do we know who speaks so convincingly of what 'I' know and believe? Do we understand who is giving these messages and who is responding? Are there two heads together, two voices talking, and do they know each other's voice and face?

IV Ground of Understanding

Have they talked before? If not, then how do we know how things happen?

We have no way to look for this kind of how; there are no mediators who have access to the full context of thoughts and beliefs that have arisen in mind and been developed through the ceaseless activity of mind's regime. However certain we may be of how and why we think and feel the way we do, in reality, it is more likely that we do not know. Few of us would admit to that depth of not-knowing, but is there another choice? We may not yet have enough understanding to answer that question.

Inviting the Light of Understanding

When we think our way of doing things is right, that sense of rightness becomes the foundation of our motivation, action, and interpretation. We are not likely to ask how thoughts and feelings come up in our minds or stop to reflect before we speak or act. When mind jumps too quickly into certainty, we may not pause to consider how the patterns of mind are directing our thoughts and actions. We may fail to notice that we are relying on inferences, guesses, and ideas presented by a mind strongly influenced by imposed concepts and habitual responses.

Decisions based on concepts taught to us by others are not as dynamic as decisions based on understanding that arises from within the clear light of mind. The light of understanding illumines our entire inner landscape, informing thought, feelings, opinions, judgment, and all our minding operations. Within this widely open, 360-degree perspective, patterns of mind become transparent. Confusion dissipates, freeing mind from the tricks and biases of its own regime.

Even a little understanding works like a powerful magnifying glass, allowing us to see more directly into the workings of mind and understand how we set ourselves up for frustration and pain. Guided by the light of understanding, we can connect with the natural brilliance of mind and open to the full dimensionality of experience.

43

Transforming Characters of Experience

Just as water freezes and becomes solid under some conditions, mind has densities that can thicken and produce different characteristics: agitation, frustration, anxiety, lust, jealousy, bias, frustration, and not-knowing. Mind also accommodates all kinds of wisdom, manifold types of delusion, and all their extensions and variations.

Mind generates these qualities and manifests them in shape and form through a process of perception that involves identity and recognition. Since time is required for identity to take place, and this activity cannot take place in the past or the future, identity has to operate in the fluid dynamic of present time.

This means that while our dualistic minds can present in frustrating and painful ways, there are also possibilities for flexibility. Just as snow or ice can become water when the weather warms up, the patterns of mind will melt when our mental environment becomes brighter and more accommodating. Since time influences how the mind works to generate toxic and disruptive emotions, time is the factor that can lighten the density of mind and cause mind to dissolve these troublesome patterns.

Density of Mind and the Quality of Experience

The density of mental qualities depends on the collaboration of timing, identity, and labeling. In our minds, moodiness, bias, and jealousy each have a distinctive density, as do lust and anger, both associated with red, and the numb, lost, spaced out, stoned, and totally tortured states related to dark blue and black.

How we associate these densities with mental characteristics determines how we identify, label, and relate to them. Behind the simple recognition of density are strongly distinctive associations that make such qualities as anger and love seem totally different. The mind oppressed with negativity manifests as heavy, threatening, or frozen, while the mind radiant with love, joy,

IV Ground of Understanding

happiness, and good health is lighter and more open, with densities that tend to flow smoothly.

How do we learn to associate certain characteristics with density? It is likely that someone pointed them out to us early in life, naming them and emphasizing their meaning, perhaps while admonishing strongly and repeatedly, "This is bad, this is evil, this will hurt you, no one will like you," until we accepted that this object or behavior is dangerous or undesirable and began to associate it with fear, guilt, or aversion.

Thus, how we view mental characteristics depends on how our circumstances and history reflect in what presents itself at the moment. Senses and mind contact an object within the dynamic current of present time. But, in order to identify an object, mind has to mark out a unit of time that allows recognition to take place. This action connects experience to a particular unit of time and identifies the experience with a particular label, a particular reason, or a particular circumstance that is taking place. Almost instantly, these sensory impressions are influenced by qualities that mind has already learned to associate with the label. When past associations conflict with feelings and emotions flowing in present time, we tend to react to the label and overlook

Transforming Characters of Experience

what is actually happening. This is why our reactions do not always match up perfectly with the experience that is manifesting in present time.

Although experience unfolds as a continuum that includes such manifestations of mind as joy, love, hate, anger, dullness, resentment, creativity, positivity, health, happiness, and well-being, our minds tend to break experience into segments that it can identify as positive, negative, and neutral, depending upon how mind has been conditioned to view them. Marked out and identified, they become fused to our concept of past, present, and future.

From this basis, mind establishes associations that include our self-identity and personal characteristics. Among these characteristics are both negative and positive assessments and behaviors that can manifest in very dynamic ways. On the negative side are frustration, anxiety, withdrawal, depression, and varieties of disabling neuroses. On the positive side are affability, tranquility, serenity, calmness, and clarity: accommodating qualities that are less bound up with problems, fears, and worries. Developed and stabilized, such positive qualities establish the conditions for balance and harmony.

IV Ground of Understanding

When we consider how mind interacts with time to isolate segments of experience and identify their characters, we begin to see that the qualities and characteristics that manifest in our minds are directly related to those that manifest in our being. In turn, the qualities of our being also feed back to mind and influence our state of mind. This understanding may inspire us to consider how our ways of judging and evaluating specific, frozen units of experience may be exposing us to a needlessly heavy burden of negativity. As understanding melts illusions concerning the nature of time, our attitudes, thoughts, and actions will also manifest differently, affecting the whole of our inner and outer environments.

44

Relief for the Restless Mind

Our minds are now strongly bonded to a dualistic operating system, so we perceive and think within that perspective. Pressured by time, uncertainties, and desires, vulnerable to confusion and pain, we have no choice but to live within the limitations they impose. But the qualities of spiritually developed beings reveal the possibility of an alternative way of living. If we were confident that we had the same basis as they do, if we knew our minds could manifest the same beautiful qualities, we could take inspiration from their example and release our self-doubts and anxieties.

Perhaps these beings once had problems similar to ours and lived as we do today, working through the same struggles, even if on a much more advanced level. When we admire the qualities they embody and contemplate their beauty, wisdom, and the power of their love and compassion, we project their beauty and love into our

IV   Ground of Understanding

refuge, fearing to expose insights or feelings that are too sensitive to share.

Viewing Problems as Opportunities

Understanding can be the best form of knowledge. Called forth to observe thoughts and emotions in new and liberating ways, it can free us from the self-centered interpretations, stories, and emotions linked to mind's system and to its custom-made language. Instead of searching for reasons and explanations when a problem arises, we can go directly to the center of the problem and observe it, watching for what we may have misunderstood. We can ask mind directly, "Is there something I did not understand? Is there something that has been overlooked? Is there something that needs to be understood?"

This way of questioning merges into mind's inner dialogues and taps into its feedback loops of identity and interpretation. Instead of recoiling from the problem or pushing it away, mind engages it, perhaps even eagerly, with energy and interest. The concepts 'misunderstanding' and 'problems' take on new meaning when we see how they enable understanding to take place. Mind eventually concludes, "Yes, there are problems, and I welcome them, because I need them to be free of misunderstanding."

When mind embraces problems as opportunities for understanding, we become students eager to learn, and we know that there is something to be learned. As we recognize what we have misunderstood, understanding takes care of the problem. When another problem comes, we have some positive momentum that can sweep us past initial resistance and open our minds to alternatives we may otherwise have dismissed. Understanding is at work, almost without our noticing. We can work with that dynamic to accommodate more understanding.

The first level of understanding is the level of not-knowing, where we blindly follow where mind leads. This is understanding manifesting as not-understanding. The second is the level of intelligence, where we recognize our lack of understanding. A third level is the knowledge that comes through questioning and observing how mind works, how it demonstrates subject orientation or object orientation, and how subject and object relate to one another. Observation invites understanding and encourages it to develop. If we continue to observe how mind operates as we go about daily life, beyond that third level we may

IV Ground of Understanding

find another, more spiritual plane that can in turn open to still higher, more all-encompassing fields of understanding.

Once we are on the path of understanding, we will notice when we are uncomfortable or when we did not understand. When we have made a mistake or caused a problem, whether or not we are aware of our role in the problem, understanding will give feedback, and we will not need to repeat it. When we feel that our knowledge is not sufficient for a situation, we can take note of this feeling also, and understanding will come. Every step of the way, we can take heart from the knowledge that, whatever problems come up, they are simply reminders that understanding is not yet complete. There is still more to be learned.

Eventually, it may be possible to bring understanding very close, before the point where mind marks up time and the cognitive process begins. Here, before the problem takes hold, before misunderstanding and emotions can grip head and heart, understanding can immunize mind's system of recognition and interpretation, the entire minding mechanism, the psyche, and even awareness against the negativity perpetuated by mind's regime. In time, we may experience the higher purpose of understanding: To take care of

Relief for the Restless Mind

problems all at once, instead of coping with them one by one.

Without understanding, we would have no choice but to remain the way we are. But the more widely we open to possibilities in all directions, the more understanding reveals itself and the more dynamic it becomes. We do not have to be in a certain place or strain to reach for some higher knowledge. Whatever mind we have, however we embody it, that is the right mind to use and the right place to be. That is the place to accommodate understanding.

45

Steps toward Understanding

Understanding takes hold most readily when we are prepared—when we are relatively free of self-doubt and receptive to what presents itself to be understood. As preparation, it may be helpful to envision ourselves connected to a greater cause, the movement toward understanding itself. Our task is to recognize misunderstanding and transform it until no problems remain.

Preparing for Understanding

Wherever we stand right now, we have arrived at this place because we understand something. Our understanding is greater now than it was before, even if it sometimes appears to manifest as misunderstanding. We continue to move toward understanding, realizing that there is always something new emerging and much more remains to be understood.

Steps Torward Understanding

Without taking any position or point of view, understanding leads us on a journey that continually unfolds new dimensions of experience. It activates inner capacities for knowing, awakening a deeply energizing sense of aliveness. As it manifests in our experience, we embody the lighter, brighter way of being it enables. More aware of the treasures within our own body and mind, we become wiser, open to positive qualities, but free of the need to chase after joy, bliss, knowledge, or enlightenment.

Understanding provides what is needed. As understanding begins to inform our thoughts and actions, we may be more comfortable in our embodiment, at peace in body and in mind, with no pressing problems to resolve.

Actually, there is only one major problem—not understanding. There is also no problem at all, because there is understanding. Someone who does not understand has a problem, while someone who understands has no problem. The one who understands and the one who does not understand may seem to be in opposite places, but both can be students and practitioners of understanding. As long as we have a problem, we are in the problem camp. When we graduate from

IV   Ground of Understanding

the problem camp, we no longer have a problem. But without problems, we may not graduate, since we do not have anything to understand.

Starting with No Understanding

We can start by asking what we need to understand. Whoever does not understand can begin here—at the point of no understanding. Does understanding have to do with mind? With objectivity? With unpredictability? With time? With our lives? With universal existence? Yes, understanding has to do with all of these.

As we identify and label each problem, we can also determine who is looking for understanding. Going on, we can question how labels relate to meaning, and ask, "Who is making decisions? Are there conflicts?" It helps to look further and identify the nature of the problem. Is misunderstanding the problem? Is it that we do not have knowledge?

When we look at each step of the process, we understand that any problem has different aspects. Perhaps our environment, culture, language, or previous experiences contribute to the outcome of our problems. If we become unhappy, for example, we can explain why: the

Steps Torward Understanding

story is available. We are responding as mind has directed. But we do not know the whole story that led up to the experience of unhappiness, and we do not know all that has influenced our reaction. Understanding even this much, we know that our minds and 'us' have some issues to resolve. We still have something to understand.

46

Imitations of Understanding

As long as our mind is playing games, we are fully involved. Activated by the urge to express, mind's energy flows through our patterns of identity and response, ensuring that whatever words or actions result reflect our custom-made language. Our mind is loyal to this language, as well as to the labels and meanings it generates.

Understanding means depending on what has not been understood. But if we try to do this by relying on our custom-made language, we reverse the meaning of this advice and misunderstand how to proceed. Grappling with mind, we think "I have to understand what is going on." Then mind says, "I understand what you need. I will search for it." Not realizing that we are only interacting with mind, we participate to our full capacity, urging mind on in its search. This is no pose: We are fully involved, a sincere, fully engaged student of understanding.

Imitations of Understanding

> Two people go to court.
> One stole a sheep
> and the other did not.
>
> Both deny stealing the sheep,
> but one did and one did not.
>
> If mind does not claim to own
> the truth, it is a fact.
>
> If mind plays games, saying,
> "I have right understanding,"
> this is not the truth.
>
> The truthful one is not the one who lies.

Mind can imitate the truth, saying, "Now I understand." But this is only a word game, and words alone do not hold the truth. Since the pattern is strong, we take on this falsehood without realizing what is happening. But other tests are available. If we are not free from fear, if we are not free from pain, we have no understanding. If we are attached to right understanding, and think, "Now I have it," we have taken ownership, and ownership is not right understanding.

How Mind Undermines Understanding

We can make distinctions between higher understanding and lower understanding, full understanding and limited understanding, authentic

SECTION FIVE

LADDER OF UNDERSTANDING

If we are still labeling certain life situations as 'problems', we can be sure we are still subject to mind's regime. Confused and dense, our 'problem mind' is mired in 'not-knowing', Understanding refocuses the mind and guides it to a different way of operating.

Activated "before the point where recognition takes place and establishes linear time," understanding offers a ladder into a freely-flowing realm of unbounded light. Within that fully liberated understanding, it may be possible to connect with the authentic quality of being.

47

Finding the Right Track

As soon as we identify a situation and label it as a problem, we need to question the character of our response: does it come from interest in what the problem might be revealing? Or, are we aware of the uprising of impatience, frustration, or some other impulse that is prompting us to deny or avoid the situation? Understanding guides us directly to ask: How is mind working with this circumstance? How is it judging and responding?

This approach to understanding, which applies to all situations, helps clarify whether we are on the right track. It embraces interpretations based on past experiences, then goes further, taking into account all the factors, internal and external, that have come together to produce this particular result. Incorporating both subjective and objective aspects of experience, understanding is comprehensive and fully inclusive. Recognizing that each experience is unique in its own way, understanding leaves nothing out. Understanding operates globally, at once enfolding and transcending conceptual knowledge and the meanings conveyed through language to reveal directly how things occur and how they work. It illuminates the entire mechanism of mind: how it operates, who is supporting it, who is interpreting it, who is governing and directing it, who is making decisions, who is accepting decisions, and who is identifying and assigning the labels.

How Mind Hijacks Understanding

Mind's regime can play along with understanding, commenting and agreeing: "Witness this. Yes. That could be a problem. Yes. Look more closely. Yes. Getting pleasure. Yes. Making progress. Yes." In seeming to accommodate understanding, mind is actually stalking it. Subtly inserting itself in the process, it is shifting the central focus to ME. ME: having a problem. Yes. ME: working on it. Yes. ME: depending on my mind for progress and improvement. Yes. With this, we have come full circle: the mechanisms of mind are once again in charge.

Mind hijacks understanding the instant we begin tracking the thoughts that it generates. Its retinue points here and there with advice and

V Ladder of Understanding

comments that distract us from the unfolding of understanding. "Look here; no, look there. There is something else you have not looked at, something else you have not yet considered."

Where did the idea of 'something else' come from? And what about 'there is', which seems to suggest, "Perhaps I have been repressing something important." 'There is...' seems so strongly imprinted in mind that it comes forth reflexively in thought and speech. Mind says yes, IS. IS becomes a mark that establishes IT IS, validating and pinning down what mind has identified. There IS. There IS NOT. Yes. No. Decisions made by mind are put forth to be voiced and upheld by the central director, variously named I, me, and mine. This is how mind—and no one else—makes the laws by which we are supposed to recognize reality.

Mind establishes the parameters and guidelines for thought and action, and educates us on how best to follow them. It is as if mind has made a list of things we have to do. Now it is presenting that list. "You should wake up, you should look at this list, you should think about it, you should do something. You are important because you have all these jobs to do. You should fill large

Finding the Right Track

notebooks with lists and carry them with you wherever you go. Now you are ready to do business. Now you can accomplish something."

There is a speaker here, and somebody has already empowered it to direct us. Who is that empowering agent? Isn't that mind?

Mind continues, tirelessly playing its role, occupying us with trivia, distracting, nagging, reminding, tormenting, and torturing us, top to bottom and point to point.

"I need to answer this call or that letter. I need to do these errands. But why do I feel so much urgency behind these minor tasks when there is something more important I want to do?"

Mind does not reply, but continues on its track: "Do you have the list? Are you carrying it? Are you working to get your jobs done?"

There is the one who directs, and there is the one who does. Thinking we are in charge, we may never notice the one who directs, because it is designed into the system.

We only have the list.

48

Deactivating Dualistic Mind

Understanding can apply externally or internally. The external application has a small, particular focus: on the need to deal with confusion, for example, or to clear up unfamiliarity. The internal form of understanding is analytical in nature: it applies to everything involved in mental activity, including sensory presentations, identity, recognition, labeling, subject and object. It analyzes the workings of mind, taking into account everything involved in the process and how each aspect relates to the others. It also takes note of pro and con vacillations that flicker through inner dialogues, associations, interpretations, and other minding operations. Ultimately external and internal become aspects of the same understanding.

When we become familiar with each aspect—the subject orientation, the object orientation, mental processes and interactions, and any positive or negative impressions that affect our

Deactivating Dualistic Mind

attitude toward problems—we have a broader foundation for understanding. Then understanding can be more universally applied.

Now we are faced with particular situations. Let's say we are confused. As soon as we note confusion, we can activate a way of dealing with it. Something resolves, and the problem no longer exists. This is also understanding. However we label these approaches—analytic or theoretical—either approach effectively solves the problem. It does not matter what we call it as long as it results in understanding.

Problems Fundamental and Specific

Our fundamental problem is that we are operating within the limitations of the dualistic customer mind. The antidote to that problem is understanding. For what purpose we need the antidote, exactly how it helps us, is irrelevant at this point. At this level, the most important understanding is that we have the ability to help ourselves. Understanding solves the problem by revealing the deceptive assumptions that underlie it.

Different problems come up every day, at any time and at any place, throughout our lives. Today we have a problem, and we resolve it.

V Ladder of Understanding

Tomorrow another will come, and again another and another. As long as our minds are operating, they call our attention to problems that may be lurking at the edge of our awareness: "I am angry, I am frustrated; my co-workers are jealous of me; I am totally lost, emotional, and depressed; I am in pain, I am lonely; something is missing in my life. People don't like me. My boss takes advantage of me. Everyone expects too much out of me. No one listens to me or supports me. I just have no energy. I want to do something else. Why can't I find the kind of work I want to do?"

Since we are supplying all the ingredients for problems, problems come up automatically, and the reaction will come, because our minds are prepared to produce the expected response. If these kinds of problems persist even when we know that the antidote is freely available, this indicates that we are still playing roles, still using our customer minds and custom-made language.

Problems will continue to arise as long as we allow our minds to relate to situations in this way. But when we understand that we are the ones identifying and responding, we may be motivated to step back from the problem and take a second look. If we do this before the urge to respond results in action, the identity of

Deactivating Dualistic Mind

'problem' may not arise so automatically, and we may experience a lesser response. Then a similar situation comes, and we go through the same process until the urge to respond weakens more and finally goes away completely. Noticing the change, we may wonder how we could have let our minds trick us in this way.

These are the mind-rhythms with which we are playing. Seeing how they manifest is the first level of understanding.

Understanding Brings Release

When the patterns of our problems are as familiar as our own images in a mirror, the instant they manifest, we recognize that a familiar pattern is repeating. Recognition brings understanding: since we know where it leads, we can take a step back and look again from a different position. Seeing the situation freshly cuts the momentum of emotion, allowing space for understanding to arise. As soon as we embody that understanding, the problem releases. When the problem drops away, there is nothing left to understand. Instantly, we know. That is what knowing is.

49

Understanding Accommodates Our Way of Life

Understanding embraces sound, words, and concepts, then expands into deeper levels of mind, where it awakens gratitude and appreciation. Gratitude softens rigid attitudes, and appreciation deepens understanding, making it ever more clear and direct.

The process begins with the realization, "Aaah—I misunderstood." This is the beginning of understanding: We realize that there is something to be understood. As our focus shifts toward understanding, we see with new eyes and feel our spirit buoyed by the arising of understanding. Each step is the start of a new experience: recognizing misunderstanding, looking freshly, then allowing a new understanding to brighten our being. Now we understand what we have never understood in quite that way before.

These moments are opportunities to carry understanding even further. Has something been

Understanding Accommodates Our Way of Life

overlooked? Are there more problems remaining? If mind is bringing up frustration or discontent, some kind of sadness, or a sense that something is just 'not right', we know that there is something to understand. We can continue to broaden the range of understanding by appreciating how skillfully understanding releases problems as they arise.

Up to now, we have been absorbing and mastering the patterns of the concept-bound mind, taking them in completely and without question. Anything we can say or think about has been labeled and fully established. Our patterns are now totally and solidly real, and we are continuing to learn and extend this way of being through our thoughts and actions. We could learn to accommodate understanding in this same way, inviting it to open each and every pathway.

Expanding in all directions simultaneously, like the glow from a luminous globe, understanding bathes mind in light until no not-understanding remains. Eventually nothing is left to trouble our being—no dark clouds overshadowing mind, no hidden knives poised to stab the heart, no thorns growing secretly inside to irritate the spirit.

V Ladder of Understanding

Secret Beauty of Understanding

Understanding is a rich embodiment of knowledge, the birthright of human consciousness and our most precious human heritage. An unfailing source of warmth and inner joy, it accommodates our way of life and fulfills the deepest needs of body, mind, and spirit. It clears away confusion, brings harmony to thoughts and senses, frees mind of biases and the heart from regret and resentment. Cultivated and respected, it remains a faithful companion throughout our lives, enriching us with beauty and sustaining us in goodness and compassion.

Understanding removes obstacles and allows all positive qualities to manifest. Self-revealing, it operates simply, without fanfare, while finding expression in wondrous, even magical ways. Our being responds with humility and appreciation that arise spontaneously, free of manipulation and untainted by obligation. Our present time becomes lighter and more wholesome, our actions more joyful and helpful to self and others.

Up to now, we have bought into the dualistic framework of mind. Forced to choose between acceptance and rejection, we have had no opportunity to recognize and embrace the infinity of alternatives that the awakening of understanding can unfold. Now we can turn this orientation on its head and learn to act with eyes wide open. Everything that was created through not-understanding can be reversed and redirected through the liberating power of understanding.

Taking hold at the frozen core of misunderstanding, where our energy is most tightly confined, understanding melts the bonds of attachment, insecurity, and fear, releasing energy that flows freely through body and mind, and washing away any residues of misunderstanding that may remain. Understanding allows our being the freedom to flourish, free of attachment to things we cannot control, free also of the need that drives us to control. Always with us as a supportive and calming presence, understanding works from within by engaging the regime of mind and neutralizing tendencies that push us toward agitation and anxiety. Manifesting as confidence that accommodates and transforms, understanding leads to openness and inner peace.

Looking in this way gives us access to the liberating unfolding of understanding. Sensing its power to release confusion, anxiety, and emotional turmoil, we can be open to its warmth and

V Ladder of Understanding

enjoy, and participate in the drama, responding effectively, even compassionately, simply by appreciating the unfolding of understanding. At this stage, we become candidates for a higher level of education, prepared to observe experience in a way that invites more understanding. We might call this the post-graduate level.

It helps to realize that extending understanding is part of an ongoing process. Although a problem may be solved for the moment, providing a basis for further understanding, there is a tendency to revert to the same patterns of identity and re-cognition as before. But leverage improves with experience, enabling us to deal with problems more effectively. When understanding has unfolded more fully, the negativity underlying the problem completely dissipates. There is no suffering, no pain, and no confusion; our mind has not become neurotic or unbalanced. At this stage, the change is more lasting.

If we ask, "Has understanding taken care of the problem for the rest of my life?" that is not so certain. If we lack the attentiveness and equilibrium to maintain understanding, we may forget what we understood and reweave the threads of our previous attitude. We may still fall back into our old patterns and play again the same way.

What Does Understanding Do?

Understanding removes misunderstanding. If we stumble on a hornet's nest and get stung, we will experience pain. But the next time we will know not to walk that way again. If we had that understanding earlier, we would not have stepped there in the first place and that pain would not have happened. In this and in any of our life situations, understanding instantly provides the knowledge that prevents pain from arising.

Understanding frees us from dependence on approval of others. However others criticize us, we have the confidence to take our own direction and come to our own conclusions. If others insult us or use language that is demeaning, we understand that is their way of asserting the superiority of their position. Now that we are protected by understanding, we may sense the insecurity that prompted this behavior. Guided by compassion, we may be able to respond more appropriately and effectively.

Understanding enables us to see the truth of our situation more clearly. When we think we see a snake, we may react in ways that block understanding of what is actually present. With more understanding, we may realize that what

V Ladder of Understanding

appeared to be a snake is just some kind of puppet—a stick, perhaps, or a rope, and the initial shock soon melts into relief. In time, we may still perceive what appears to be a snake, but, knowing it is only an image, a kind of television show, or even just a transient electrical pattern, we will not have the same reaction.

It may be that the reason for seeking understanding is itself not real. There may be no problem with this. If the problem does not occur to you, then no question arises. If there are no questions left, we no longer have that problem. We cannot imagine unimaginable problems, precisely because they are unimaginable.

51

Acknowledging Misunderstanding

What are our best ideas prior to the moment of recognition? From the point of recognition forward, we have only mind-made designs, stamped with mind-made concepts, processed and interpreted using custom-made language. These concepts are not even entirely our own. Just as dollar bills printed at a few government mints are used by people all over the world, we are essentially recycling concepts and ideas generated by others, using them as the basis for still more concepts. Although our minds have shaped them to our situation, this shaping was done through the filters of our limited understanding. In this sense, we could say that all mind-made expressions and interpretation come from misunderstanding.

As concepts and ideas grow in number, our ability to identify new problems of mind also seems to be increasing. While it seems that peo-

V Ladder of Understanding

ple in ancient times had fewer problems than we do, it is also possible that their languages had not yet developed concepts to identify and express them. As language changes and terminology continues to become more particularized and complex, the nature of our problems also seems to be changing. From this perspective, we might wonder if the proliferation of ever more precise concepts is somehow connected to the proliferation of problems in our world.

Constricting Influence of Complexity

While human beings have been developing their minds within this same framework for thousands of years, it is possible that this approach to knowledge is no longer serving us well and may even be contributing to a decline. The more we rely upon it, the more complex becomes our world and the more confusing and uncertain our lives, with more problems and fewer solutions.

The tendency to hide from our problems only increases these difficulties. The more clever our efforts to present ourselves differently or avoid discomfort, the more we teach mind to play games. As we repeat positions, backtrack, add, revisit, and revise, we are sharpening mind's

Acknowledging Misunderstanding

tendencies toward multiplicity. The patterns planted in mind tend to extend themselves and become more ingrained. Obstacles accumulate, intensifying confusion, until we find ourselves living in a tight, knotted realm. The program becomes our reality, not for just an hour or two, but continuously.

If all concepts, expressions, and interpretations of mind come from misunderstanding, misunderstanding is the problem of our problem, and it has to be understood. To do this, it is necessary to investigate the fabric of misunderstanding, see how the threads of the fabric are confused or disrupted, and allow them to be rewoven by understanding.

Infinite Clarity or Infinite Ignorance?

Problems involved with mind may be general, affecting our overall state of being, or specfic, manifesting as pain, agitation, blocked energy, or confusion. When we attempt to analyze such problems conceptually, we tend to confuse them further, because of the way our minds identify and process information.

As soon as mind identifies an object, we have a reference point that can be discussed and

V Ladder of Understanding

elaborated. Similarly, once we identify a problem, we can continue to describe and interpret it, building it up with conjectures and explanations into something very concrete and important. The harder we strive to clarify a solution, the faster and more cleverly we may build up something simple into a mass of complexity. The more substantive content we feed back into a mind predisposed to multiplicity, the more problems we are likely to generate. Mind hears whatever we express, processes it through identity and perception, and makes it real through feedback, repetition, and associations.

Talking about problems may only intensify confusion. It seems as if the more we talk, the less and less we can understand, because this is not the way that understanding operates. Understanding that depends on words and concepts established by mind is not the understanding that interests us here. Since reliance on concepts intensifies the minding business of mind, striving for infinite clarity—through infinite proliferation of concepts—might be leading in the direction of infinite potential for confusion and misunderstanding.

Deeply involved with language and the minding business of mind, the conceptual process

Acknowledging Misunderstanding

that we rely upon for accumulating knowledge may actually be undermining our ability to cultivate, exercise, and communicate wisdom. Similarly, thinking a problem through, relying solely on the intellect to figure it out, we are not likely to find a satisfactory solution. Just as a finger cannot touch its own tip, the mind that identifies the problem may not be able to contact the aspect of mind most capable of solving it. But we can resolve the problem with understanding, because understanding that arises spontaneously goes beyond the 'pro and con' of our ordinary minding processes.

Although our human mind operates within a dualistic framework, it has an affinity with wisdom that suggests there may be other possibilities for exercising our capacity for knowledge. As long as that capacity remains, mind has the power to activate it. Although our senses and concepts now carry us in a different direction, these are our instruments for knowing, and we can only use what they provide.

V Ladder of Understanding

Inviting Understanding: How We Begin

The process of inviting understanding begins with pointing directly at the problem created by misunderstanding. Pointing out leads mind to recognize that there is something to be understood. Just as a mirror presents your physical identity, so mind shows identity of form, identity of image, identity of cognizing, identity of acceptance, identity of recognition, identity that you are aware, and the identity that presents reality. Identity becomes your reality.

From time to time, you may think you do not understand; you may think you are confused, or that you may have misunderstood. But this, too, is knowledge. If you welcome this knowledge and investigate the subject that is misunderstanding, understanding can unfold and manifest its power to transform.

Understanding asks, "How does the subject contact itself?" If there is no contact, the subject cannot pronounce anything at all, and the meaning behind the label is empty. Other ways of framing this might be, "Can you contact mind before it recognizes the problem? Is there a basis for confusion before the problem occurs? How does identity happen? What is the mecha-

Acknowledging Misunderstanding

nism that communicates recognition to recognition? How does mind contact mind?" These are advanced ways of questioning that may lead to more complete understanding. From one perspective, it can take eons of study and practice to fully understand such topics. But sometimes a kind of understanding emerges accidentally, and that too can be helpful.

52

Miracle of Understanding

Understanding eliminates all obstacles and takes care of whatever has not been understood. It opens a new frontier, where everything is understandable and there is something to understand. When we perceive that there is something to understand, even that glimmer of understanding can ease distress. Now we can pay attention to what has been misunderstood and take care of it.

When we observe the reflections of familiar patterns, it is possible to project where they will lead. Observation informed by understanding can reveal the corrosive effects of self-centered thought and mindless action. It can also clarify confusion resulting from misguided notions and behavior that lacks kindness and warmth. Sustained by understanding, self-observation can go even further, revealing and penetrating accumulated layers of bias and mistaken assumptions as well as residues of anger, resentment, paranoia, and unresolved emotions.

Miracle of Understanding

Misunderstanding feeds agitation and aggravation. But understanding reverses all that has been built up through misunderstanding, releasing tension and pain and allowing energy to move without restriction. Even when mind's energy is thoroughly engaged in wild thoughts and raging emotions, understanding can restore inner calmness and free mind to look at the situation in a new light.

Penetrative Challenging

The very situation that blocks and frustrates us may be challenging us to exercise our abilities, wake up our energy, maximize our capacities, and lift ourselves up to a more fulfilling level of maturity. Like martial artists, we can use understanding to maximize and focus inner strength. Fully engaged, knowing there is something to understand, we can penetrate minding that clouds our awareness and bombards us with concepts and emotions.

It may seem almost miraculous that in one brief instant, even in one sixteenth of a nanosecond, we could understand and thus dissolve troubling circumstances that are now so strongly embedded into the patterns of our lives. And

V Ladder of Understanding

indeed, understanding is the greatest of gifts, worthy of unceasing appreciation and gratitude.

Indications of Understanding

Recognition of misunderstanding rarely occurs easily at the outset. But for every misunderstanding, there is a before and an after, as well as a middle. Invoking understanding, we can ask, what happened, how did it happen, how could it happen, and how could it be made not to happen? Going further, we can question who was involved, and when and where it took place. What happened before it occurred, and what was the situation as it was occurring? With this in mind, we can take the next step, asking ourselves, "What have I not understood? Is there more to be understood? Is more understanding needed?"

You may notice the changes understanding brings only by observing your reactions during times of stress or pressure. Emotions and thoughts may not come up so strongly or hit so hard, allowing you the opportunity to see more clearly what is happening. The reaction is less, or perhaps the reaction does not come at all.

Sometimes it is possible to detach enough to observe what is happening in the midst of the reaction. You can feel your familiar physical responses, but they do not engage mind the same way or lead to the same consequences. Eventually, you may look back with some surprise, noting that an event that once upset you no longer calls forth a response. In time, even the memory of the underlying pattern may dissipate in the warm glow of understanding.

V Ladder of Understanding

Reader: There seems to be a magical connection between time and the way mind experiences time or projects an illusion of time.

Author: In debating these subjects, we are really fooling ourselves. Mind is all these illusions.

Reader: But I have had the impression that it might be possible to understand. This is not necessarily liberating, but it seems a good first step. The question is, how do I get out of this all-pervasive illusion? When I slow the process down, I can see the slip of the magician's hand. Is it enough to see this fabrication, or does the seeing itself become just another readout of mind? How do I ever completely cut through the illusion?"

Author: These are important subjects. Why have you ignored them up to now?

Reader: How can I ignore them when I don't see them? From all directions, I hear that this is how I am supposed to be, this is what I am supposed to do. 'How' this and 'how' that— I cannot escape this how, because this is how I am supposed to be.

Author: Exactly. That is how you surrender your intelligence and creativity and become dependent on your customer mind for validation.

54

Why We Need Understanding

As soon as we interpret, we are the customer, ready to buy, wanting to own, ready to comment, to manipulate, to be tricky. We are already involved with something. We have something to name, something to add to reality, and something to believe.

We can believe and act on anything we can imagine. But what is the first element? Where did this all start? We are not sure. Nevertheless, we suddenly find ourselves giving statements: "Yes, I heard this." "Yes, I did that." "I know that . . ." The comments and explanations immediately come forth, but we have no clue about how the transition from not-knowing to knowing happened. We may ask how it did, but it seems that we do not need the 'how'. It is too late: we have already explained it. Now we have to believe that our knowledge is based on reality. But what

V   Ladder of Understanding

mind is presenting is little more than echoes of its own process.

What Needs to be Understood

Mind programs the system and produces the product, and mind receives and confirms what has been produced. Within this system, mind activity manifests as sensations, thoughts, identity, recognition, and more to generate the illusion of continuity. Needy and desperately insecure, mind may recycle and revise a perception multiple times to convince itself that the illusion it has created is real. But perhaps mind cannot create reality; perhaps it can only create illusion.

Recognition validates, and validation certifies what has been cognized, then establishes it as truth. From that point on, mind occupies us with one program after another. Love, compassion, merit, wisdom, the spiritual path, analyzing the nature and problems of conditioned mind—each merges seamlessly with the next, hijacking what little understanding manages to emerge, with no break in between. Even our struggle to understand and move beyond programs can become part of the program.

Why We Need Understanding

Since there has to be a subject for mind's truth, mind recognizes 'I'. 'I' am the interpreter and judge, and mind is the agent. 'I' and my mind are much the same. Mind validates truth, so these meanings cannot be dismissed.

Mind constructs logic and makes reality. It carries on with this creator role through its way of interacting with the senses. Discriminating between good and bad, like and dislike, mind authorizes labels for everything that can be named and provides the language to express these labels. Mind projects the illusion of certainty and strength, for we cannot dismiss what our senses and mind tell us. But the illusion can evaporate if mind is overburdened.

Even when mind becomes chaotic and disoriented, the image of 'I', me, and mine remains. We still experience mind as the creator-principle and 'I' as the owner and dictator of mind.

Easing the Programs of Mind

Actions based on emotional complexities drive the momentum of mind's programs, but they may not be functioning the way we thought they were. As understanding engages these programs, ingrained patterns do not work the same way,

V Ladder of Understanding

and we may glimpse the possibility of a different way to respond. The games and projections continue, but they weaken. As the programmer function becomes less central and the regime of mind less assertive, we may realize that 'I' is more of an arbitrary concept than an inflexible identity. Now we have opportunities to act more independently. We can question mind, and when we do, we discover that the process of programming is not necessarily so locked-in and automatic.

Meditative contemplation may help relax the hold of identity and the emotional complexities it sustains, showing us how to use mind in a better way. New possibilities open, offering choice. There are teachings we can apply to keep from slipping back into unhealthy patterns, and such help is useful at this point. But if we lack understanding, these practices may not produce the desired result.

Understanding refers to understanding all aspects of conditioned existence: how it works, how it operates, how we create it, and how we make ourselves victims of our own creation. What we think and do is important, and it is necessary to understand why this is so. Since we are training our minds with each thought and

Why We Need Understanding

action, we need to consider carefully what the consequences of this training will be.

When we observe our thoughts from this perspective and reflect on our experience, understanding will gradually lessen the force of mind's programmed patterns, relieving us of certain kinds of confusion and pain. Each pattern that releases its hold frees the mind to accommodate more understanding, powering a new interaction that invigorates and uplifts. Subtly yet steadily, like a flower opening in spring, a new way of being emerges and manifests through thoughts and actions. Then we can embody the benefits of understanding, so that others can see them and realize they too can free themselves from cycles of expectation and pleasure that end in disappointment, regret, and remorse.

55

Ladder of Understanding

Microscopic examination of our physical body reveals layer after layer of structures and movements—cells, intracellular structures, elements, molecules, atoms, and nuclei—invisible to the naked eye. If we had a way to magnify the inner realm of mind, we might find similar layers or stages. Observing the deeper dimensions of mind, we might note different characteristics and patterns of energy manifesting from stage to stage. If we knew how to look beyond the surface of mind and enter even the first of these stages, we would have a key for understanding different aspects and levels of our mental operations.

Limitations of Positioning

We tend to relate to mind's most dominant aspects, those that govern thinking and calculating on the one hand and the psychological levels of emotions and feeling on the other. But if

Ladder of Understanding

we go to a different level, thoughts, perception, and other minding operations might take different forms. Even past memories and future projections can manifest in different ways and call forth feelings that vary in intensity. How many more possibilities might be potentially available?

For now, however, mind is limited by the very nature of the perceptual process. For example, adopting a point of view or taking a position seems to be built into the processes of perception and minding. Such positioning happens instantly and automatically, even instinctively, without our knowing. Although we may not have been aware of taking a position and may have no reason for maintaining it, we tend to hold on to it and fix it in our minds as 'right'. It can become so 'right' that we would fight to defend it, perhaps even at the cost of our lives.

The tendency to identify and bond with a position reinforces it, leading us to assume that it is correct and totally unassailable. But understanding does not accept this assumption; instead, it asks for its foundation. It reminds us that we need to know what lies behind our views and opinions, our notions of what is real and what is not, what is normal and 'right' and what

V Ladder of Understanding

is abnormal and 'wrong'. Reasons may spring to mind, but reasons only move us further away from the source, further along the chain of perception, where interpretations and 'pro and con' come into play.

Even acknowledging the possibility that we may not know the answers to such questions can be confusing. It is as if we were keeping something secret even from ourselves, protecting an unknown and vulnerable part of our being, where we are uncertain and insecure. But if we understood this confusion, that particular problem would disappear. We would be more comfortable, less likely to become defensive, to doubt ourselves or second-guess our decisions.

The Natural Thrust of Mind

Positions impede understanding. But if we understood how mind operates, how its processes interconnect, how it points out objects and labels meanings, we would realize that understanding is the primary agenda of our mental capacities. Knowing that this agenda of mind is more important than any position we could take and feel compelled to defend, we can open up windows to more subtle levels of mind. Mind could become

Ladder of Understanding

our partner, revealing its depths through the momentum of its own processes. As understanding broadens and deepens, we may gain access to a realm of mind inconceivable within our present way of knowing.

We have emphasized that all our mental operations, emotions, attitudes, discrimination, and other minding qualities come through a mind constrained by its own regime. But there is another side of this operation—non-discursive, non-discriminative, non-dual, and non-conceptual: neutral, totally open, and in balance. Even a preliminary understanding of this aspect of mind could provide the key we need for going further, not linearly, one step at a time, but vertically, extending our inquiry directly into new dimensions of mind. It could be the first stage of a ladder of understanding, a ladder capable of infinite extension.

Where would we place the ladder? The right place would be before the point where recognition takes place and establishes the present in linear time. Here, at the very ground of becoming, we might find a tiny gate into a way of knowing that is not flat and one-dimensional, nor fixed on one point, but totally interactive among all

V Ladder of Understanding

dimensions of being. Seeing through that gateway, we may find it possible to activate an entirely different way of understanding, one that does not depend on time, mind, mental processes, subject orientation or object orientation. It would be a way of understanding that does not belong to anyone or anything in particular.

The further we could extend the ladder of understanding, the more our view would broaden, revealing landscapes of mind previously unknown, where even greater understanding could develop. Fully extended, the ladder of understanding might engage an unnamable quality, self-sustaining and self-illuminating, vibrant and alive with unbounded light that is not part of any kind of perception. Within that fully liberated understanding, it might be possible to connect with the quality of being itself.

Unbounded Light

Where ordinary perception is bounded by particulars, self-luminosity is not limited by the grasping of mind, by identities that label and recognize, by ignorance, or even by the unknown. Uncontainable, it has an awakened clarity that comes

Ladder of Understanding

from not taking a position. But it cannot be freely accessed until we have full understanding.

Since we do not know the whole of our situation, we cannot just leap to that perfect understanding by an act of will. This is why it is important to take understanding seriously. Received with gratitude and appreciation, understanding extends infinitely. It stays with us, a continual source of wonder and delight.

56

Obscurations of Mind

We may call understanding by different names—realization, release, wisdom, liberation, and more; we may associate it with peak experiences or ecstatic transport. But all these names refer to different kinds of perceptions, labels that point out meanings cobbled together by mind and senses, flavored by feelings and thoughts and augmented by the feedback loops of imagination. Based on this, we interpret: "Yes, this way of thinking or contemplating is rewarding; that one does not seem to go anywhere." We continue repeating the cycles of rewinding and identifying.

Once we begin identifying, re-cognizing, interpreting, and rewinding, we twist and turn, going on and on with no resolution. We are moving sideways, playing with the retinue of mind, but we are not penetrating the label and connecting with the meaning that underlies it. Our access to meaning is second-hand, an association established through the process of minding. Just seeing the truth does not take us beyond these ways of minding.

Effects of Not Knowing

Our usual way of thinking and acting creates obstacles; obstacles become hindrances, and hindrances cast shadows. We live amidst those shadows, deluded victims of desire and aversion. Disappointed, we may resort to blaming ourselves or others. But most of our obstacles have been created by this mind, operating through patterns that developed long ago. In following and carrying out these patterns, we are automatically—and unknowingly—subjecting ourselves to punishment. Who is inflicting this punishment? No one other than our own minds.

As long as we accept without question what comes out of our mental processes, we cannot avoid this kind of not-knowing. At one instant the customer mind is urging us on; at another, the business mind is marketing and selling. Now mind seeks to please, to ingratiate, to avoid conflict or pain, but in the next instant, it may

V Ladder of Understanding

edge of our own minds and hearts. The topics presented here point to deeper meanings than words alone can convey, to understanding that can come alive only within our own experience.

Beginning now, we can reverse the programmed dynamic of not-knowing. Without grasping, without allowing ourselves to be distracted, we can take serious steps toward understanding and reflect on how it operates. Wherever mind is moving, we can look for openings that grant access to freedom.

Time moves quickly in this illusion-realm of mind, and we may feel pressured. But as long as we are not ignoring or denying understanding, understanding will help us connect with time's creative power. When we are free of the constraints of dualistic mind, there will be no need to hurry, for time will reveal itself as the unbounded, infinite openness of being. But until we fully embody this understanding, we do need to hurry: Our lives are passing and the light of understanding will not shine for us forever.

57

Gift of Understanding

Understanding carries the gift of knowledge, the gift of light, and the gift of companionship directly to our hearts. Blessed with these gifts, which shine from the center of our being, we become bearers of knowledge and truth. From there we can engage the lineage of understanding, the lineage of realization, and the lineage of awakening. It is a privilege to have this opportunity to exercise understanding on behalf of sentient beings everywhere.

Understanding is the very backbone of our power as human beings. It is the light that makes true freedom possible. It wakes us up, brightens the mind, and shows the way to liberation. Supported by understanding, freedom of mind leads to vision, vision leads to wisdom, and wisdom illuminates the way for generations to come.

V *Ladder of Understanding*

Clearing Away the Shadows

Understanding shines directly into mind; clearing away the basis for separating self and other, it does away with the orientation that isolates, distinguishes, judges, and puts down. Unfolding from within, understanding clarifies the unknown and reveals the unknowable. In the clear light of understanding, there is no more darkness or entanglements. No more do we have to cope with the sense of being lost, the sense of being lonely, or the sense that we are unworthy. A mind free from these shadows can exercise the gifts that understanding offers: light that reveals the beauty and value of human life, and knowledge of the way to transmit it.

When our understanding is limited, our intelligence and creativity work against us, and our lack of flexibility automatically creates blockages in our path. But all such difficulties also create opportunities to climb the ladder of understanding and benefit from the positive qualities that understanding brings to our experience.

Once understanding unlocks our habitual ways of perceiving and opens the subtle receptors of mind and senses, mind's mechanism of identity and recognition can put words in the

Gift of Understanding

service of understanding, letting us reflect until there are no doubts left. The witness to its power is mind itself, now able to rest in clarity and peace, out from under the shadows of confusion.

As thoughts continue to drift through mind like clouds, whispering, stirring up sensations and feelings, understanding opens new channels for insight and appreciation. We may feel our minds brightening, engaging with greater interest in whatever life presents. We may notice a new ease and presence shining through our experience, broadening joy and sustaining us in equanimity through the most difficult of times.

Anyone can cultivate new areas of understanding and open new points of access: understanding language, understanding meaning, understanding time, understanding self, understanding mind, understanding the psyche, understanding behavior, understanding obstacles, understanding lack of understanding, understanding how misunderstanding makes obstacles. Through understanding, we involve ourselves in the full dimensionality of experience. We enrich the quality of our lives in everything we do, for everything is relevant to understanding. Our present experience becomes a way of experimenting with what

V Ladder of Understanding

we understand, and daily life becomes a celebration that feeds back into experience. Uplifted and inspired by the revelation of experience, we can create a meaningful realm of beauty, just as a skilled artist creates a landscape with sweeping strokes of a brush.

Expansive and creative, understanding has its own kind of charisma that attracts mind as nectar attracts butterflies. It shows the way to pay attention, and it nourishes mind. What has not yet been understood can now be freshly engaged and understood more fully. Self-revelatory, understanding stimulates and accommodates. Assimilating all problems, it resolves and transforms them into expressions of beauty. It applies in any circumstances and to any situation.

Understanding is our journey with others, an example of the gift that understanding itself makes possible. The outcome of our understanding can be reflected to friends and family and to all beings, now and in the future.

58

A Ceaseless Unfolding

Understanding unfolds all of its integral qualities simultaneously in the manner of a mandala, extending itself in all directions of space and through all dimensions of time. The field of understanding also expands, becoming a realm where understanding continuously presents new possibilities. It expands not only linearly, but also vertically and in depth, through sensing and sensitivity, through points, through any kind of physical and mental experience, through thought, imagery, and feelings. Since every point carries the three times of past, present, and future, the unfolding of understanding continuously replicates the qualities of the three times. Yet understanding is not repetitive, halting, or boring. It has little to do with the linear way of accumulating knowledge bit by bit. It is experiential, growing, and unceasingly responsive to whatever time and mind bring into being. Each point presents something to be understood.

V Ladder of Understanding

Without going anywhere, understanding embraces and unfolds as it extends. It carries on infinitely, going not towards something, but beyond conceptualization, beyond the limits of what can be understood. Extending the expansion of experience into infinity, understanding transcends dimensions of time.

Understanding never stops; it is not defeated, it never ends, it does not become tired, and it is not diminished. It is not a black hole that absorbs everything and gives nothing back. With or without disciplined effort on our part, understanding reveals itself and brings resolution. Nothing remains that could hinder or stop it. Once set in motion, understanding continues to unfold for as long as mind manifests.

Section Six

Revealing Understanding

Understanding is our human birthright. To claim it, we begin by learning to track back the 'how' of experience and gently observing the mechanisms of mind that rely upon identity and the rigid structuring of linear time. "Up to now, our only agent for knowledge has been mind; all that we know has come to us through mind. But the understanding that completely takes care of misunderstanding changes all this. Revolutionary and transformative, understanding is an entirely new process that leads us to the limits of dualistic mind and points to what lies beyond."
—*Tarthang Tulku*

59

Tracking Back the How

Sometimes people who try very hard to live up to high standards of conduct become concerned that they are falling short of their expectations. Individuals who are committed to strict codes of discipline are similarly vulnerable to thoughts that they may have neglected responsibilities or inadvertently engaged in injurious or self-centered actions. Sensitive to this kind of negativity, mind picks up on these feelings and integrates them into its minding regimes.

As a result, even the most sincere and dedicated individuals can feel pressured by self-doubt and worries, by self-blame and fears of inadequacy. When these feelings come up, the patterns of mind work against us, preventing or delaying resolution, and external gestures of sympathy may only intensify the pressure. Even concepts that express rich spiritual teachings can engage negative patterns and create obstacles to study and practice.

Tracking Back the How

By refusing to support the tactics of mind's regimes, understanding relieves deep-seated patterns that are otherwise difficult to transform. It has no need to blame or reject, and it does not ignore, avoid, or deny, Unfolding from within, it gentles the turmoil of anxiety and fear, softens the edge of panic, clears away the messy residues of apprehension and worry, and eases mind into balance.

Understanding develops through seeing the how: how mind compounds, how mind accepts and adopts, how it feels and pronounces, how it recognizes, how it identifies, and how it produces the result. Understanding allows us to see the whole context of cause and effect. Understanding the cause automatically alters the effect, turning it toward a more positive outcome. Where we may have been experiencing a painful situation, we now understand that there is no basis for pain. Receiving the signal 'no pain', mind instantly relaxes. This is not a matter of replacing 'bad' feelings with 'good' feelings. Painful feelings simply drop away, because mind is now responding to a different situation. The pain is gone, perhaps even without our noticing.

Dualistic mind is strongly bound to cause and effect, prone to blaming, scolding, and instilling

VI Revealing Understanding

guilt, directing the force of its negativity inward as well as outward. But understanding allows us to declare ourselves innocent and set ourselves free. Seeing how mind works—how it processes, compiles, and compounds to create the entire landscape of our experience—brings clarity that dispels confusion. The way to clear up problems is through fully understanding the circumstances that produced them. Such comprehensive understanding comes about from knowing the how.

Since cause and effect have to do with the how, understanding the cause—the 'way how' something happens—instantly shifts the focus of mind and directs it to produce a different result. In this way, the how can be applied as an agent of understanding. In seeing how our problems come about, we invite understanding and renounce the victim's role. Operating within the densest shadows of mind, insight into the how continually extends the ladder of understanding.

Finding the Way How

We all know the question, "How come?" Now we extend it by asking, "How does this come about?" We see through the tightly woven fabric of mind, identity, and language to understand how all

Tracking Back the How

these threads are interconnected. Tracking the way how, we take a major limitation of mind and use it for understanding.

Our familiar use of 'how' is mind's way of affirming that "I don't know how," a trick that provides us a seemingly acceptable way of avoiding responsibility and placing it upon others. But when it serves the purpose of understanding, 'how' becomes a way to wake ourselves up and see how we have been deluded, how we have misunderstood, how we have lost opportunities, how it did not have to happen that way.

Even in situations where someone else seems clearly to blame, we can ask, "How was I not aware of this problem? How did I not know?" "How did I ignore or dismiss it?" "How did I misunderstand?" Then we can turn the problem around and track it back to see how it came about. As we do this, understanding takes place.

Tracking back the how allows us to see the cause and effect, the circumstances, the theory, and the practical implications: the present situation, what came before, how the circumstances came about, and how they have been compounded up to now. Before, we may not have known or acknowledged that there was a problem we were

VI   Revealing Understanding

involved with in some way. Now we see how we are involved, how we have in some way enabled the problem to arise. We can ask how this has come about, how we may have been distracted, and how flashes of insight may have been dismissed. We might recall that excuses were taking form in mind even before the problem came to light, a certain sign that on some level we were missing a precious opportunity to intervene. When we see how we became confused, or how we overlooked some key aspect of what was happening, we have opened the door to understanding.

When we become more familiar with the relationship of mind and time, we can expand our inquiry. We can ask, "How did I identify what was happening in the present, how did I dismiss the gateway, the point that was my opportunity to see correctly and choose a better outcome?"

Summarizing the How

Once we have a way to understand problems sequentially, we can come at a problem from both directions: first asking how it came about, then applying the how to clarify whatever misunderstanding remains.

Tracking Back the How

'Tracking back the problem' may seem almost self-evident. We may realize we are emotionally involved, but not know how we became so involved. This is where we have work to do. Whenever we have a problem, we can point to a sequence of circumstances at work: identity, labeling, recognition, language, words, thoughts, feelings, emotions, and so on. Examining these circumstances, we can ask how we got lost. "At what point—identity, labeling, recognition—did I go astray? Could it have happened differently? Where was the opportunity to intervene?" Once we understand that process, we know when it is repeating and how we have been deluded. "Now I understand how I became confused. I see how I dismissed it, and how it is that I am having so much pain and suffering." Seeing this, we understand how. We can take advantage of this how for understanding.

How We Misunderstand

Misunderstanding perpetuates itself because the process of perception is pre-programmed and all the elements we need to identify wrongly are immediately available. Labels are prepared, ready to go at the first flash of identity and recognition. If mind jumps too quickly, it may impose the

VI Revealing Understanding

When we can say, "That is how I created the situation," the problem dissipates, leaving no residues of defensiveness or emotional distress, no clinging to the problem with one hand while pushing it away with the other. The mind becomes clear, fresh, and bright, ready to go on. For those who have experienced its results, this practice is truly brilliant, a perfect display of understanding.

Understanding liberates, but it does not necessarily make us a cozy home. The benefit may be that we are less tense and anxious, not lost in the tangle of confusion. What more can it do? Understanding releases pain, worry, and recriminations, so that these miseries no longer remain. We have no more problems! What more could we want?

On the other hand, it is important not to anticipate a specific benefit or a possible reward. Understanding takes care of the problem, but if we grasp it wrongly, if we seek to possess it, manipulate it, or use it for personal gain, it will slip through our fingers and disappear.

> Problems, patterns, ignorance, unknowing—
> all these former sources of pain are now
> inspirations for tracking back the how,
> removing the shadows that have
> dimmed the clear light of mind.

60

How We Understand

At the outset, we assume that we know our own minds, and there is nothing to be understood. Our mental patterns are so thoroughly established that it can be difficult even to realize that we have a problem.

Then there is recognition: "I may have a problem. I have been identifying myself with the patterns of my mind and the feelings that come up. How did that happen?" "That is my reality and I have been coping with it, but it has not solved my problem."

In a way, we already understand. We are tracing mind, we are tracing identity, we are tracing time, and we are tracing the fields of perception. In response, we are pointing out, generating reasons, expressing them, and making problems for ourselves by imprinting them on mind. Frustrated, we may suddenly realize that this is the way our minds operate, and all we do simply per-

VI Revealing Understanding

petuates these patterns. "There is no resolution, no solution, no alternative. None. None. None. Now what happens?"

Identity, Language, Time

To go further, we need to master how identity, language, and time work. From time to time, it is important to refresh our memory of where our present ways of understanding have gotten us. By reviewing these topics, reflecting on them, and analyzing our experience, we can appreciate how thoroughly misunderstanding permeates our present way of being.

Everything we know comes to us through mind—the same mind that names and establishes meanings and assures us that there is nothing we can do. Understanding comes from seeing this entire situation. Only when we see how completely we have misunderstood can we fully appreciate the value of understanding. Yet each time we identify any area of misunderstanding, we know that understanding is taking place, and we know that we can stand on that knowledge. We know how to look and how to understand, and we can use this knowledge to cultivate more understanding.

How We Understand

"Aaaaah, that is why I am in pain, that is why I am in trouble. Now I can see why I am frozen, why I cannot move, why I cannot be free." This is the beginning of understanding. At this point we can track the how back, and climb a little further up the ladder of understanding.

With each new step, we may realize, "Because of misunderstanding, I have had difficulties and experienced frustration and confusion. But now that I understand how these came about, I can allow understanding to take care of the problem."

Where do we find this exceptional knowledge? It comes from mind, from the same mind that created the problem through relying on the linear process of cause and effect. As a simple example, suppose I am depressed. The mind offers reasons, telling me that this depression is caused by someone or some event beyond my control. But now I understand that this answer came from misunderstanding. I misunderstood, I misinterpreted a situation, and I responded wrongly. Now I track back the how, and the depression goes away. How? Through understanding.

If we had not made friends with understanding, we would never have been able to track the how of the problem and make it go away. We

VI   Revealing Understanding

would have identified with the problem; we would have accepted it, compounded it, and continued to hold onto it, perhaps with growing desperation. But now, because of understanding, mind lets go, because the problem no longer has any substance or reasons that mind can relate to. If we could not identify with problems the same way, if we did not defend and enforce them with reasons, might problems manifest differently?

Understanding gives confidence and comforts body and mind. It sets up a pattern that dissolves the roots of misunderstanding and makes room for greater understanding to arise. In time, we can trace the problem back not only step by step but instantly, capturing the whole minding process. Eventually we can take on all of our problems at once.

Following the how of mind, self, and I to its source, we can understand how the fabric of our reality came to be woven. Then we can take advantage of all problems life throws in our path. We can allow understanding to weave our experience into a living, embodied tapestry in which problems cannot arise.

Whatever we have treated wrongly, we can now set right by applying this model of how and

How We Understand

extending the ladder of understanding. The more we see the need for understanding, the more spontaneously understanding arises, and the greater becomes our appreciation and gratitude for this opportunity to witness its unfolding.

61

Benefits of Understanding

Once we understand how mind works, the benefits of understanding begin to unfold. We are no longer strangers to ourselves vulnerable to self-doubts, insecurity, and fear. We know the territory—we are familiar with the way mind identifies and seals up perceptions; we are clear on how mind interprets and the way it projects. Knowing that we have a tool for handling anything that comes to us, we are confident in our ability to extend our capacities for understanding.

Understanding brings comfort and protection, freedom from surprises and torments inflicted by habitual patterns of response. There may be a sense of lightness, a release of agitation and fear, and a brightening of attitude. There may be a deep sense of gratitude as we realize that we are more genuinely self-sufficient. No longer afflicted with the need to imitate others or copy their approaches and style, we can communicate

Benefits of Understanding

freely, confident in our own experience and the power of our mind.

Embracing All Experience

The quality of understanding remains with us, a source of reassurance that we are no longer a slave to whatever thought or emotion mind produces. Protective tensions relax, and conflicts that create separation arise less frequently. Just as drops of water touch and merge, distinctions between body and mind, ourselves and others soften, and interactions become more harmonious.

No longer welcome, confusion, fear, self-doubt and other negative emotions lose their power. Once they have been recognized and transformed on the inner cognitive level, it may not be necessary to conquer them completely. We may have the option to neutralize them and redirect their energy into insight and compassion.

When mind no longer grasps, identifies, and elaborates through reasons and interpretations, the inflow and outflow of habitual reactions even out. Seemingly difficult situations arise less often or even vanish entirely. Understanding shines through our actions and communicates to others, awakening understanding in them also.

VI Revealing Understanding

Enriched by their experience, understanding reflects back to us, establishing a feedback loop that is positive, energizing, and supportive.

Detaching from the Drama

Understanding enables us to see through appearances and sort out what lies behind the manifestations of mind. We might think of mind as a skilled actor who is caught up in the drama and continues to play it out. But the audience is none other than ourselves—we are the ones recognizing, identifying, and responding. If we are suffering, this suffering is just another aspect of mind's display—our reaction to the actor's skill at deception.

If there is no audience—if we do not participate—the drama cannot continue. Now the actor can be questioned directly. "Does this drama have any foundation? Is this real? Or are these simply manifestations of my mind, associations from the past, completely unrelated to what is happening now?"

The ability to question in this way allows us to take advantage of mind's own processes. For any kind of feedback to take place, mind must recognize and identify what is being shown. Here,

Benefits of Understanding

at the point where mind stops to re-assess and re-interpret, a space opens between the actor's presentation and our response. This gap provides a valuable opportunity for choice and re-direction.

Since mind's actors can wear different clothes, appearances can be deceptive. When mind unexpectedly presents us with a fearful image or impression, someone who believes that the image is real responds instantly. Someone who has more understanding may think, "That image seems very real, but it has no basis." That person may be affected much less strongly, and whatever fear comes up may not last so long. A third person, one who no longer plays the part of audience for mind's drama, may not react at all. He or she might not even notice this machination of mind.

Whenever we feel fear or strong emotions, understanding enables us to look again, asking "Is this situation really what it appears to be?" The forms or words that before seemed so threatening may turn out to be little more than puppets, messengers that carry thoughts and images, but have no real basis.

If there is no audience—no 'I' to be drawn into the drama—perhaps there is also no theater and

VI Revealing Understanding

no stage. If there is no audience and no place for these forms to dance, perhaps they are merely projections, powerless holograms that can dissipate like mist in sunlight. When that is our understanding, we know there cannot be a subject and an object. But we also understand why someone runs away when there is no snake.

Is the Ladder 'Real'?

Does understanding 'occur' or not 'occur'? Unless it occurred, we could not draw upon it. But it has no starting point and does not occupy a place. It unfolds in all 360 degrees of experience simultaneously, just as light illuminates a dark room upon the flicking of a switch.

Those advanced in understanding can look from all possible points of reference to question the subject of mind itself, or the senses, cognition, or the presentness of the present. Questioning is carried in the presentness of the present: this 'presentness' is the bridge that brings forth the meaning of the cognition. While the intellect has no way to question the nature of this 'presentness', an embodied understanding, one that does not depend upon subject and object for rec-

Benefits of Understanding

ognition, knows that presentness is the foundation for the ladder of understanding.

Is the ladder itself real? It depends on our point of reference. If there is no reference point, we have no way to set up the ladder and move forward. If we do have a point of reference, we are starting from a subject/object orientation and subject to its limitations. Even so, the ladder is helpful, a vehicle we can extend to ascend more quickly to higher levels of understanding.

62

Self-Mastery Through Understanding

We live as consumers in the realm of desire. Our eyes are consumers, our tongues are consumers, our ears, noses, bodies, and minds are consumers. All the senses cooperate, reaching out to objects in our surroundings and advertising them to us, showing us how attractive they are, how important and useful, how meaningful, and how necessary to our happiness and well-being. Mind convinces us how right we are to take pleasure in what attracts the senses, and how right we are to desire them. "Yes! This is true, this is good, this is right."

Our way of being is based on the senses and their ability to give pleasure, which in turn stimulates desire and attachment. The proof is everywhere: in the care people take for their physical appearance, in their way of dressing, their behavior, their speech and their gestures. Since all of these behaviors engage the senses, we tend to emphasize them when we wish to make a good impression. Mind accommodates and supports this seductive quality, which extends to art, to music, to social interactions—to nearly anything in the entire fabric of existence. We find ourselves responding, "I like that; I want to have it."

This same receptivity to attachment also bonds mind to sources of pain and torment. Here too, understanding gives leverage. Bondage itself can help us understand how to approach the problem effectively and how to cut the connection.

Moving Toward Freedom

We can begin by understanding the pattern of one troublesome quality, such as anger or obsession, or any other feelings rooted in attachment. Seeing where it leads, we can track it back to determine how it developed and where it began. We can also turn it around, tracing from its origin to its full manifestation in our present experience. Then we can transfer what we know about that pattern to another quality, then another and another.

At first, we will continue to see the drama manifesting and feel our reaction. But later we can use the leverage that understanding provides and apply it to the reaction itself. Who is the

VI Revealing Understanding

owner of this fear or emotion? Who is responding to this sensation?

"I understand that the root cause of my reaction and the impulse to act comes from my notion of 'me'—I need to protect 'me'. But what is presenting a danger to whom?" When we ask where fear is occurring, the focus goes to the responder—'me'. But 'me' can also become the subject, and then an object is established. Eventually we may understand that the object of the fear could just as easily become the subject. This kind of reversal can also be applied to other situations.

Examining experience in this way allows useful glimpses of new understanding. We could almost say we are observant in a new way, more fully aware of the interaction of perception, mind, and language. Knowing how to observe and analyze experience, we develop the leverage necessary for lessening the force of habitual patterns and begin to free ourselves from the need to repeat them.

Balancing in Understanding

We want to know how the mechanism of mind works: How does mind, the knowing one, cognize? How does its way of cognition determine

Self-Mastery Through Understanding

the quality of our lives? How does its mechanism take us over so completely? We could sidestep these questions all of our lives, always staying at the same level. But then we would be an imitation of ourselves, repeatedly acting out the same reflections of our minds.

Understanding is actual, living life-experience. It has the power, by quieting mind, to inoculate us against the 'dis-ease' of meaningless repetition. Relying on understanding, we can ease confusion and neutralize frustration. Able to balance feelings and emotions, we can make this mind more peaceful and accommodating. We may even reach the point of equilibrium, where there is no separation from compassion, loving-kindness, and joy. In all these ways, understanding brings relief and speeds our steps toward higher levels of understanding.

A New Way of Understanding

Our embodiment is an orchestration of mind. On behalf of mind, on behalf of all aspects of our being, we need to know how our embodiment interacts with mind, how mind relates to mind, and how 'I' and mind communicate. Even if we think that there is nothing to be understood, we

VI Revealing Understanding

can look more closely at mind and trace the features and stages of our mental processes. We can take a journey through perceptions, recognitions, and interpretations; we can enter the regime of mind and track it as it goes about its business. We can engage the realms of memory and imagination and listen to the endless dialogues of mind with mind. All this mental activity shows us where we stand. Then understanding speaks for itself.

The journey of understanding—how to be, how to manifest and extend the interactive quality of mind and the universe of cells and organs that constitute our embodiment—has an important role to play in the life of every human being. When understanding begins to free mind from the confused labyrinth of minding, emotionality, and self-interest, the human spirit awakens, leading naturally to a more comprehensive understanding. It is not necessary to define or systematize this revolutionary understanding, or even to wait for it to develop. It is already present in some form, and it will manifest when we know how to look and how to question.

Understanding is light that transforms mind darkened with repetitive thoughts and hungry

Self-Mastery Through Understanding

for truth. When it arises, everything is completely clear—nothing is left out.

> Before, I was in a state of not understanding.
> Now I understand that I did not understand.
> I did not understand my mind, but now
> I am not looking the same way.
>
> Now I can make distinctions between knowing and not knowing. I know now what I did not know before. Now there is knowing based on understanding mind.
>
> I can trust that.

63

Guidelines for Understanding

Understanding is not our possession or our property. It is completely open, above, below, and within. It surrounds and encompasses everything. Nothing is excluded.

From the start, it is important that we appreciate understanding and allow it to extend itself naturally, without attempting to own it. If we treat understanding as our property, if we make it our understanding, or grasp it as a tool we can use to solve our problems, we will freeze it. If we think of it as 'my knowledge', or 'my understanding', we will confine it within the realm of self-orientation, where it can only operate within the limitations of mind's regime. Imprisoned in this way, understanding becomes dogma.

While understanding does not belong to us, we can belong to understanding. In order to engage it, we must allow it freedom to expand. We do

Guidelines for Understanding

this by letting go of wanting to know or demanding to understand. As we release our hold on understanding, appreciation shines forth, allowing understanding to reveal its inner depths, like a lotus flower or a mandala that unfolds when conditions are right. Appreciation continues to strengthen and extend understanding. Viewed with humility and respect, freely available to all, understanding can give rise to a lineage of knowledge that will continue as long as there are those who understand.

Protecting Access to Understanding

Respect and humility keep open the gates of understanding and activate its power. Without them, understanding remains just another concept that points to, but cannot convey, the joy of continuous becoming that heightens awareness and enlivens experience.

We protect our access to understanding by allowing it to unfold and grow. Set free of concepts and definitions, understanding shines ever more brightly, dissipating the shadows that tend to accumulate around perceptions, labels, and concepts. Totally unbiased, understanding embraces positive and negative alike. It neither

VI Revealing Understanding

applies nor requires any antidotes. When even misunderstanding stimulates the expansion of understanding, what can inhibit understanding? When the light of understanding is everywhere, misunderstanding no longer exists. Perhaps it never did.

Up to now, our only agent for knowledge has been mind; all that we know has come to us through mind. But the understanding that completely takes care of misunderstanding changes all this. Revolutionary and transformative, understanding is an entirely new process that leads us to the limits of dualistic mind and points to what lies beyond. Never linear, never confined, understanding unfolds continuously, expanding in all directions simultaneously.

64

Understanding Beyond Mind and Time

Generally, we divide understanding into two types: knowledge that applies to the objective 'real' world and knowledge that relates to the subjective realm—two components of understanding that relate and communicate directly with one another. But both aspects of this kind of understanding operate within the realm of our dualistic minds. Whatever is cognized—whether subjectively or objectively—is projected through mind. The subjective realm is set up by our projections, and so too is all that takes place within it, including the instruments, the measurements, and the entire frame of reference we call objectivity.

Not yet awakened by understanding, the subjective mind treats the objective realm as concrete, solid, observable, reliable, and predictable, to be examined and interpreted as 'real'. But the objective realm also arises through mind.

VI Revealing Understanding

An All-Encompassing Subjectivity

With few exceptions, Western science and philosophy have not emphasized that all observation takes place within mind, that awareness and sensing are within mind, that measurement and readouts are made by mind, and that even the instruments we use are mind. Yet a model that views measurements and observations as objective does not take into account that such tools and methods also belong to mind's projections and can only be interpreted within mind's field of understanding. Mind is the one that frames and observes; framing creates the field of mind, and mind's observation takes place within it. How can mind not be intimately involved with the knowledge that results from this way of observation?

When we observe, we take in a reflection of the object, impressed into mind by our way of naming and conceptualizing. Mind has established all these details, labels, and concepts, even before the division into subject and object. In one sense, 'objective reality' is a game mind plays. Seeing only the final moves of this game, we accept its conclusions as absolute and real.

Within mind itself, the emotional mind and the conceptual mind reflect and feed back to each

Understanding Beyond Mind and Time

other. Mind encompasses both fields of activity, including all our ways of philosophizing as well as scientific observation and discovery. Without mind, we cannot interpret; without mind, we cannot observe, and without mind, we cannot input and feed back.

The way pronouncements are made, the way feedback develops, and the way results show up are also mind. Nothing in this process—input, experience, observation, feedback, understanding, or knowledge-ability—goes beyond mind. No one can bypass mind to discover knowledge that is free from its imprint.

Scientists say, "We discovered that phenomenon. This is our knowledge." But isn't it mind that discovers? Isn't mind the one that cognizes and confirms the discovery? All that led up to the pronouncement "We discovered," came about through the operation of mind.

So far as we can observe, mind is the instrument for any field or discipline of knowledge. Without mind, we cannot discover or know anything that is within the realm of mind, not even such seemingly huge and remote subjects as space, time, and knowledge. If we were to discover something outside the realm of mind and time, it would inhabit a different dimension and have different

VI   Revealing Understanding

characteristics. It would be an entirely new phenomenon, and it would exist in a different way. In that case, could we discover it after all?

Understanding Leads Beyond

Although we emphasize the importance of rightness and truth, we have not emphasized the extraordinary value of understanding. Perhaps we assume that it is commonplace and mistakenly take it for granted. To appreciate the power of understanding and bring it alive in our being, we need to know how it operates and who operates it. We need to know what understanding is and what there is to understand. We also need to question when and where we are to understand.

While language can point beyond our present understanding, it cannot follow where understanding leads. Understanding may extend far beyond the realm of mind, beyond our present time, beyond our present way of observation, into dimensions we have never seen or explored. It may communicate subtleties that lie beyond the capacities of our mind to observe and comprehend, beyond its ability to conceptualize and express. Within a different view of time, these applications of mind might not even apply.

65

Knowledge-ability of Understanding

When we can track back the how, we have a new kind of feedback system, one that does not just recycle what has already been built up. Informed by a fresh perspective and open to a different understanding, we have a second chance—we can re-cognize whatever has happened and find out how it happened. Tracing the history of what has happened reveals a body of manifestations that are outcomes of our minds. Now we can investigate sideways, forward, backward, or some other way, asking what is really going on. Looking in a more direct way, we may learn something new.

Feedback that leads to deeper understanding looks at who is reacting or who set up the story in the first place. A message has been understood, but we may forget to consider the one who understood it, the one in whom this understanding arose.

VI *Revealing Understanding*

Extending the Ladder of Understanding

Going close to the source, gathering all information possible, we can arrive at a form of understanding we might call 'simple knowledge'. We would like to know more—we would like to extend our knowledge and invite more understanding. To do this, we need to see exactly how understanding is related to knowledge, and we need to understand the know-ability of knowledge itself. Understanding and knowledge may be parallel; neither can safely be denied or ignored.

Knowledge by its nature is open; this means that there is always something to know that we cannot dismiss. Knowledge determines what is known, what is knowable, and how to know. Understanding calls knowledge forth, informing it and empowering it to unfold organically, in a way that unifies intellect and experience. It opens our angle of view more widely, giving us access to broader fields of knowledge.

Wielding the weapons of not-knowing, ignorance, and denial, mind tells us, "You cannot know, you cannot receive, you cannot have this information." But understanding ignores such boundaries. Embracing subject and object, positive and negative, understanding heals and

Knowledge-ability of Understanding

restores, making our knowledge whole. Without understanding, there is little chance that knowledge would be universally beneficial.

The beauty of understanding is that it has knowledge-ability, the ability to bring forth knowledge from the unknown as well as the known. In this knowledge there is no rejection, no ignoring, and no discrimination. The beauty of its ladder is that it extends ever farther. Negations are its rungs, steps that lead us to a higher plane, where knowledge unfolds without limitations. Understanding awakens a true love of knowledge, and knowledge, in turn, embodies understanding.

We must not forget that we already have access to the ladder of understanding. Knowing this, we need to remind ourselves from time to time, "I will not reject understanding or ignore it. I will not procrastinate, saying 'I will understand later, not now'. I have had enough pain. Now that I understand how I have been enslaved, I wish to come out from under the dark shadows of mind. I refuse to accept that there is something I cannot know. I want to participate in the unfolding of understanding."

VI Revealing Understanding

There is nothing we cannot think about or know, nothing we do not have the opportunity to understand. If someone claims, "But there is nothing to understand!" we can just say "No!" This assumption is not a stopping place. When we hear it, we can be certain that there is indeed something to understand.

"It may be true that there is nothing to understand," we answer, "but I want to look anyway: at the meaning, at the concepts, at who said what, at what that means. You may convince a simple person to give up, but knowledge is never naïve, and I refuse to be naïve on its behalf. I am ready to extend the ladder of understanding. I am ready to defend the source of my freedom and the way to knowledge."

On the other hand, if someone says, "I have the ultimate understanding! This is the ultimate truth, there is no need to look further!" My answer is the same. "Why do I have to stop here? I want to understand more! The understanding I aim at is all-inclusive. It puts everything on the table."

The options are boundless: to understand not understanding, to not understand understanding, to misunderstand understanding. We need to extend the ladder to its fullest, incorporating

Knowledge-ability of Understanding

all possibilities into every stage. Where knowledge may now be very partially open, it can open to a full 360 degrees. Where we may now understand three dimensions or four, the ladder of understanding extends beyond them. We can extend it even farther, deep into realms where subject and object do not apply, where there is truly no more to understand.

66

Freedom of Understanding

Some may say, "I do not understand," as a way to assert their power and avoid responsibility. But by rejecting understanding, they have only committed themselves to not-knowing. We need to ask, "Why should I ignore what is happening? Why should I accept rejection? Why am I ignoring what is happening and giving rejection so much power? Why not let go of misunderstanding instead?"

Letting go of misunderstanding instantly lightens up any situation. How does this happen? Perhaps we understand that in projecting understanding, mind is playing a game with us, inviting us to react according to its rules. Knowing this, we can relax and invite understanding to take place.

The understanding we are inviting is comprehensive. It unfolds as long as we remain receptive; it does not define boundaries or point out

Freedom of Understanding

where to stop. It expands until very little not-understanding remains, and that also we can eventually understand. Empowered by such a reliable foundation, we can fully inhabit our own body of knowledge and manifest it to others.

Supported by the ability of knowledge to arise and develop under its own momentum, the extension of understanding does not lend itself to distortion or manipulation. Understanding continuously feeds back into itself, supporting more understanding. There is no meaning lost, no empty promises given. It absorbs and collapses discrimination, bias, not-understanding, and rejection.

Understanding gives freedom and the fullness of joy. There is no more doubt, no more fear, no more residues of negativity. Each time it arises, it extends the range of our vision. Whatever outcomes await us at the frontiers of mind, from hardships to blissful experiences, we can embrace them in the spirit of exercising knowledge, as if we were mastering a new skill or sport. Fields upon fields of manifestations arise and fall, each one a precious expression of mind.

Exercising mind on behalf of understanding can bring great pleasure. Pleasure, because

VI Revealing Understanding

this way of being is inherently creative; pleasure, because it cannot be possessed, and still greater pleasure because it is generous and kind, able to awaken good feelings in others. Pleasure also, because of the beauty of boundless expression that can manifest to us as if presenting a magic show, vision, or dream. Pleasure also, like watching the joyous play of unborn children, or gazing upon a magnificent garden whose flowers have no roots. Mind can manifest all these expressions and more, and we can enjoy them, free of attachment and obligation.

67

Envisioning a Regime of Understanding

It is likely that the regime of mind is a product of earlier times, developed to serve specific purposes, but now too complex and overloaded to address the fundamental problems that still challenge us today. If mind had agents more oriented to understanding, it might establish a regime that would expand our vision and better serve our needs.

A regime attuned to understanding would give feedback through all the stages of cognition, allowing understanding to emerge freely within the patterns of labeling, interpretation, and mind dialogues. The more understanding, the more clear and flexible our mental processes would become. With mind less tightly controlled and locked in, a more relaxed mental environment would allow greater latitude for moving in and out of the rigid patterns of dualistic mind. Ordinary mind gives us no choice: The instant perception and thoughts come up, we are frozen into

VI   Revealing Understanding

a tight, unyielding state. But when understanding shines more brightly in mind, this tightness melts, and we can come and go more freely.

Lightening the Density of Mind

The more understanding we have, the more we can see the operations of mind's regime multiplying, expanding their own power and making mind ever more dense. This is consistent with the role we have played until now, participating in the automatic process of identity and recognition that imposes on mind a limited view of reality. But when the driving force of automatic responses weakens, mind continues to brighten and become more clear, almost translucent.

The more closely we are in contact with time—perhaps a hundred thousand times more closely attuned to time than the passing of a nanosecond—the less prominent a role identity plays and the less binding our attachment to habitual patterns. Unable to sustain its accustomed tasks, mind's regime relaxes its grip, enabling us to operate it differently. Since problems and obstacles cannot arise in such a clear and open envi-

Envisioning a Regime of Understanding

ronment, we have an opportunity to experience a new freedom of mind.

An Independent Way of Seeing

We have seen that if we trace the nanosecond to its tail, we come to a point of transition that goes beyond ordinary time, a point where identity, minding, and role-playing no longer apply. This point, the beginning of the beginning, has a special mechanism of exhilaration that reveals perspectives that the operations of mind do not ordinarily allow. We may still have our familiar way of seeing, and we may still observe it in operation, but now we also have independent seeing, independent functioning, and an independent way of behaving and doing. We do not have to act automatically.

How do we experience this smallest unit of presentness, where our ordinary dimension of time is so radically reduced? While we cannot pin down this point and mark it, we can develop a process that leads there, a path available to anyone who sincerely wishes more understanding. We can engage it in all instants, all the time, in any situation, within any possibility, all the way.

VI Revealing Understanding

Continuing to unfold, understanding may yet reveal an entirely new domain of mind, a vast, untouched wonderland that lies just over the horizon, a freely accessible realm of knowing unburdened by the busy-ness of mind and the control of mind's regime—a realm of knowing beyond any we can now imagine.

68

Revealing Understanding

Mind's boundless creativity manifests in its ability to bring out all manner of shapes and forms through a process of cognizing, feedback, and recognition. Informed by understanding, these processes become the ladder that uplifts understanding, transforming a simple process into an ongoing revelation. In this transformation, the self-revealing, liberating quality of understanding itself bears witness to the power of mind's creativity. Joined with understanding, mind's creative power ensures that understanding will continue to manifest in the beginning, in the middle, and in the end.

Nothing is outside the purview of understanding. There is nothing that you cannot know, and nothing is excluded. Understanding unfolds even within misunderstanding, encouraging an inner process of lightening, inspiration, and direct feedback. It continues to reveal itself, deepening and broadening into abundance that is all-

VI Revealing Understanding

embracing. The revelation continues even as understanding unfolds and transforms into illumination. The going is the education, and the revealing is the understanding.

Rich, open, and infinitely liberating, understanding makes the revelation happen. This revealing is not a going anywhere, but rather an unfolding that opens to all directions, spontaneous and self-directed, self-rewarding, self-educating, and self-acknowledging. An unmistakable sense of deepening bears witness to its truth. It intensifies as understanding unfolds, and knowledge emerges ever richer than before. Opening in this way, understanding reveals itself as unbroken continuity.

Pathway to Understanding

Identity introduced by linear time—by our reflexive reliance on past, present, and future—locks us into patterns that confine our being and freeze our experience. But understanding dispels the tightness of mind and melts fixed views, allowing fresh alternatives to manifest. Even a mind enmeshed in delusion can serve as a pathway to deeper understanding, revealing to observation and analysis the right juncture and right con-

Extending Understanding

nections. All misunderstanding can be loosened up by this way of understanding.

Knowing how mind's systems operate, we can release the frozen knots of thoughts, the sense of threats to self, the images and imagining so full of fear and worry. We can value all these manifestations as opportunities for cultivating understanding, for without them there is nothing to understand. All dark shadows of mind—all the ignorance, toxic emotionality, and confusion, all that is not understood—can be revealed and transformed by understanding. Whatever we most value—creativity, humanitarian benefits, a fulfilled and positive way of life, the spiritual path—understanding is there to support it.

For every aspect of human experience, there is something to understand. At every turn, we can ask: "How did I misunderstand? Where did misunderstanding originate, and by what process did it develop?" These questions are keys to understanding. Once we understand, that in itself solves the problem.

VI Revealing Understanding

Claiming Our Birthright

The way of understanding is the surest way to connect to mind and self, to reality, and to the intensity of experience as it arises at this present point of being. We have never reached that place; perhaps we have never even thought about it. Yet all this can be done, should be done, and must be done. To realize the full significance of our humanity, we have no other alternative.

Understanding is our birthright: It cannot be usurped by ignorance, and no one can take it away. A shining light and powerful inspiration for our path, it is the invincible, wholly victorious unfolding of knowledge that conquers negativity as naturally as the sun shines. In the light of understanding, there is no above and no beneath; there are no dark shadows of emotionality, no reflections of self-doubt, limitations, and loneliness. Totally free in all directions, completely luminous, understanding discloses freedom, and freedom becomes victory.

AFTERWORD

LIGHT OF KNOWLEDGE

*Introducing the
Vision and Purpose of the
Dharma College Curriculum*

An Address prepared for the opening of
Dharma College, April, 2012
by
Tarthang Tulku,
Founder of Dharma College
and Head Lama of TNMC

Dharma College Opening Address

Light of Knowledge

The purpose of Dharma College is to stimulate the expansion of knowledge by encouraging individuals to extend their own knowledge: you are all well educated, well trained, some are even teachers and masters of certain western disciplines, so your knowledge is already well developed. Further extension is nonetheless possible, and I believe the wisdom tradition of the Buddha has a unique role to play in this regard. Certain preliminary ideas about Dharma have been circulating in western culture for several decades, creating some familiarity, as well as some expectations, about this ancient path of wisdom. My approach begins with the unexpectedly simple and moves toward deeper understanding through a sustained process of dialectical investigation.

At this moment in time, at this juncture in world history, we have an opportunity to investigate and improve the way we use our mind and energy to make it more productive. Though the classical Dharma traditions do not use the term, we might call this mind and energy our human spirit. Through observation, dialogue, and closely engaging thought to thought individually as well as and mind to mind among us, we directly and personally expand knowledge. Each of us has access to extensive resources including the accumulated knowledge developed by the civilizations of the world as well as the specific disciplines we have individually studied, practiced, and used in our own lives.

Classes of Knowledge

Generally speaking, three different 'classes' of knowledge can be identified, all of which are operating in the world today in varying degrees. The first class of knowledge establishes the transmission of a discipline from the past to the future via the present. The master trains the disciple in the views and methods of the discipline, and the disciple, according to his capacity, becomes the trainer of the next generation. This knowledge is founded on our learning what has been taught to us. This transmission has produced an unbelievable extension of understanding, together with the explosion of methods, tools, and technologies

Classes of Knowledge

that we enjoy today. Improvements in our way of life, extension of life span, and control over many external circumstances are sample results of this class of knowledge, which grants us the key to participation in the worldly ways of life according to civilization's standards and patterns.

A second class of knowledge is derived from the first but begins to work out the consequences of the extension of knowledge as disciplines multiply and technical information expands. There arises a thrust toward using knowledge to resolve more subtle human problems and more complex global problems. New specialties bring about new solutions, as well as increased productivity and greater control over the physical realm.

The volume of our current knowledge has burgeoned far beyond what a single individual could possibly master in a lifetime, while it takes half a lifetime to become expert in a single field. And so it happens that a person's time and energy is devoted to mastering a particular type of knowledge, but the outcome is not completely in line with the expectations that inspired that investment; in the end, the return is not truly worth the cost. The gap between the original vision and the actual outcome becomes more obvious with this

Light of Knowledge

place within the context of this familiar realm. We inquire into the history of philosophy or science, we trace the lineage of current understanding back to great figures and founding fathers of different eras. But we do not probe deeply into the more fundamental level of what knowledge depends on, the building blocks of language, the labeling process, the making of meanings, perception, and identity. Where do these elements come from, how do they arise and operate, and what is their nature and potential?

How, for example, do sound and concept bond inseparably so that, once we learn the language, word and meaning arise together instantly? The first connections between given sounds and given meanings must have been made in prehistory. At some unknown point, once that linkage had taken place and was agreed upon, the label was no longer questioned. In fact, our knowledge depends on these linkages being unquestionably certain and clear.

As mind adopts the language system, it also adapts itself to language, functioning in distinctive new ways. Words allow the creation of identities with generalized names that can be applied to specific things. The identity becomes quite

More Fundamental Levels of Knowledge

fixed, the thing inseparable from the name that immediately invokes it. The self too has names and labels, such as 'I' and "me." The identities of our world become interwoven with the past associations of the self and its history, so that personal experience manifests a complex tapestry of meanings. But we rarely think to ask how this tapestry is woven and who is creating the designs, who is doing the weaving. When we take the patterns and the pattern-maker for granted, the possibility for deeper inquiry disappears.

If we keep the inquiry going, we might notice how mind as an identity-user locks into patterns that are oriented toward the past, the already-known that provides the label from the existing knowledge reservoir. Even the most sophisticated ways of using labels to create new concepts for cutting-edge thought or inventive e-commerce enterprise, for example, depend on words defined by previously defined words. All of our innovations rely on what is already in the system in order to extend knowledge further. This is part of the beauty and transmissibility of knowledge.

The reservoir of words is not static, however. Words come in and out of fashion; with overuse, they grow trite and meaningless; with disuse, they grow antiquated and are set aside completely. If a whole language falls into disuse or is not allowed to be used, eventually it disappears. Does this mean that the living culture in which the language was embedded is bound to fade away? Can the genius of one language simply be replaced by another language? Without a culture's native words, the meanings that reside in its storehouse of knowledge may not be accurately cognized in all their richness and specificity. We do need to understand this relationship because ancient languages are disappearing every day, and we do not even know how to measure the loss. When Tibet's wisdom tradition is translated into 21st-century English, how much meaning will be captured and how much will simply vanish without anyone noticing that something is missing?

The foundational interconnection of language, mind, and self, however does not seem to disappear; these interconnections are highly stable and seem to be present across the whole species. The operation of mind, as we understand it, is almost inconceivable without language. If experience is not 'translated' into words, we cannot comprehend it. Without the label and the patterns of the past, mind cannot connect to the

More Fundamental Levels of Knowledge

meaning and interpret it. And yet the basic link between sound and thing appears to be arbitrary. Is our entire labeling system founded on a prehistoric whim? Does our vehicle of knowledge ride on such shaky wheels? There seems to be something important here to investigate.

But this topic has not received much attention, for researchers are intent on moving forward to expand knowledge rather than returning to the roots. And how to explore those roots? Must prehistoric facts about the original linkages of sounds and things somehow be accessed? Do we need to investigate the way sound vibrations bond to visual sensation? Do we turn to the anthropologists for their best guesses, based on evolutionary explanations or go to the neurologists for their theories based on the brain mechanisms for acquiring language? To suggest that these linkages are not intrinsic, but man-made, arbitrary conventions may contradict certain religious convictions and be placed out-of-bounds for investigation by believers. At some point, we may shrug off the whole exploration as too mysterious to handle, simply beyond our ken.

Crucial Field of Study

I believe the relation between knowledge and language is a crucial field of study if our knowledge is to progress. Take, for example, the relation of the label 'I' to the self we believe we are. Can we imagine this self forming if there had never been a name for it? Are distinct 'things' born from language? Is it possible that the self is conceived by 'I' and birthed by 'me'? But are 'I' and 'me' different? This may seem a ridiculous question, and yet if we ask: Is 'I' different from 'you'? then we hurry to say "yes!" 'I am' does not mean 'you are', and 'mine' certainly does not mean 'yours'. These are important, meaningful terms for 'me' and for 'you'. Though we are the ones traveling the road to knowledge, isn't it strange that we do not know where our own names come from?

If we could move to this deeper level, little by little, and at the same time expand our scope more broadly until both the perimeter and depths of knowledge were fully embraced, nothing would remain mis-understood, and we could access global understanding. Then we could see how it has happened that the world has arrived at this particular juncture in space and time. We could ascertain the actual coordinates of the point that knowledge has reached in the 21st century. We would know where we came from, where we stand now, and in what direction we are headed.

The evidence of the Dharma traditions indicates that it is possible to look more directly into mind in ways that could liberate us from limitations. When seeing with new global eyes, knowing is fully embodied so that nothing 'other' remains outside its scope. In the light of knowledge, the presence of knowing and the knowing of presence are indistinguishable, both tool and terrain to explore, dynamically unbounded and unsourced. Knowing in this intrinsic way opens up to illumination and innovation that is untraceable to a past and unprojectable to a future. Creating the accommodating conditions to begin moving in such new directions is the purpose of Dharma College.

Purposes of New Knowledge

The thrust toward new knowledge so as to better our situation is a hallmark of the human spirit, a remarkable global endeavor that has been underway throughout our history. The great thinkers and doers of the past have placed the results of their life's work in our hands. Their texts and treatises, piled one upon another, would surely reach to the moon! Our most recent innovation, the world-wide-web and the Internet with its Google search engine, gives access to uncountable facts and puts new tools at our disposal every day. Now how shall we make use of this abundance?

It is important to be able to see clearly the overall direction in which humanity is moving, to identify the choices and decisions we must make for the sake of future wellbeing. I believe the crucial questions of our era, yours and mine, are these: How shall we use and improve our human knowledge? Toward what ends shall knowledge serve? What is the best approach to expand knowledge today?

The Dharma traditions articulate the purpose of developing knowledge that benefits self and other. 'Self' includes the mental, emotional, physical, and spiritual health of this person. 'Other' is a vast category that includs all other sentient beings and the entirety of the environment that these beings inhabit. All of these must be included and cared for if we are to sustain our health and inner balance.

Today the health and inner balance of us all seems limited by external and internal obstacles that roughen the road that we must travel; by confusing complexities emerging as cultures isolated in the past are interacting for the first time in history; and by divisiveness that hampers a person's connection to him- or herself, his or her connection to the world, as well as the connections between people and between countries.

These limits on wellbeing actually prevent the growth of knowledge as well, for knowledge and well-being are inseparable. If the purpose of knowledge is the increase of well-being, and if increasing well-being promotes expansion of knowledge, then releasing these limits would have a profound synergistic effect, catalyzing movement in new directions. Once we understand it better. we may be able to take advantage of this interconnection.

Acknowledging the Primacy of Mind

Thus far, we have been letting mind dictate to us instead of knowledge dictating to mind. In other words, we have not gained significant control over the operation of mind, which holds the power to take us in directions we do not wish

Light of Knowledge

to go. As a result, we are not able to protect our own wellbeing. Wherever mind and senses move, we follow, whether heading toward pleasure or moving toward pain. Modern knowledge, focused on externals, does not yet have ways to control the inner sphere of emotions, ignorance, disappointments, disillusionment, self-deceptions, and conflicts. Due to positive and negative conditions, and subtle kinds of cause and effect we do not detect, mind presents its patterns very rapidly, with fast variations that we can scarcely monitor, let alone control.

We might say 'I' is operating mind: reacting, initiating, and behaving. We say, "I am angry!" "I need this or that." But it seems 'I' cannot control these reactions and that most of the time 'I' have little choice in how they manifest. We cannot, for example, command mind not to bring unpleasant memories—it does bring them. And yet mind is supposedly our instrument, our agent, even when it does not seem to be on our side. Mind and self have signed and sealed a contract so long ago, we cannot even imagine breaking it.

Wherever we turn, mind is already involved—consciousness and unconsciousness, visionary moments, memories, perceptions, feelings, posi-

Acknowledging the Primacy of Mind

tive qualities such as discipline, effort, or kindness, and negative ones like laziness, pride, and resentment. Though all experience relates to mind, we do not know precisely what mind is. Mind seems shy and also sly, transient and hard to pin down, intransigent and impossible to capture. When we look at mind directly, we can find no shape or form, no top or bottom. And yet when emotions arise, mind comes alive with powerful energy that is very tangible and real. Body and senses react to the emotion, action patterns are initiated, and behaviors with distinctive characteristics take place. This entire exhibition is initiated by some unseen movement in invisible mind.

Mind transparently flows through the entire body, one of its duties being to connect to the functioning of the body's operations. On another level, mind must also be responsible for consciousness, perception, thoughts, projections, and subjectivity. Based on mechanisms such as recognition and identification, mind's functioning supports our human creativity and the fabric of our knowledge.

Without mind how could the samsaric realm be created? How could experience be received or cognized? Can we even imagine that experience is happening but mind does not exist? If there is really nothing there, then how does experience even happen? Where would we be? Who would be behind the experience, who would understand the words? What meaning would experience have if it did not connect to or relate to us? We seem quite certain mind must be there, despite its invisibility.

The Need for the Next Step

Let us imagine mind is present, open 360 degrees, completely invisible but shining, all pervasive through the body so that the point of a needle can be applied to any spot and be felt so immediately that it seems no time at all is required. Likewise, every thought form that comes and goes flows through mind, though we do not know where they come from or where they go. As thoughts shift and change, the possibility of a neutral and detached view seems to get lost in the back and forth, and a subtle sense of duty arises; there is something to take care of, and somebody must do something. Mind seems compelled to respond to experience.

An anxious grasping quality arises, and as its momentum grows, divisive energy spreads out to body, senses, memory, and consciousness, pro-

The Need for the Next Step

ducing a subtle but relentless pressure. More complex reactions such as confusion, frustration, and conflict now arise, and can increase, until paralyzed by fear and guilt, we cannot take any action. The divisive grasping may generate so much complexity that our intentions to exert discipline or hold a focus are undermined, and we just let ourselves be buffeted by the waves of whatever thoughts and emotions arise. Or intellectual mind may step in to defuse the anxiety, offering advice, or providing theories to support some sense of stability and some way of understanding of what is going on.

But at any moment, a memory comes back, a new emotional reaction is provoked, or results of actions undertaken in confused moments feedback to us—the job is not done, the communication did not succeed, the plan has failed, and so forth. We feel caught up in a messy, pressured situation that now demands even more effort and intelligence to untangle, but our state of mind has become much less confident and capable with all the confusion, guilt, and fear running in the background.

Current knowledge does not have good methods for working with mind at this level. Mind's divisive, anxious, grasping operations create conditions that debilitate intelligence and generate fear. Fear closes the heart, so that we lose our compass and even our common sense. How can we release ourselves from this pressure and use the power of mind in more productive ways that reward us with the joy and aliveness we need to nourish the human spirit? I believe we all wish to live in that state of being.

Instead of adhering to the current contract, where mind dictates and demands, and we blindly receive and react, we could appreciate our mind and energy in a new and deeper way as a partnership founded in knowledge. Then we might move in truly new directions. The negative, divisive energy could be converted to positivity that was free of all harmful unpleasantness and enmity. This precious energy, our energy, could be used in beautiful and as yet undreamed of ways.

Envisioning New Knowledge at Work

Imagine this cycle of positive feedback: If we had access to knowledge that could diminish the obstacles, the confusion, and the divisiveness that interrupt our wellbeing, we could relieve the increasing pressure toward isolation that is currently shrinking possibilities for individuals and

Envisioning New Knowledge at Work

for societies. No longer defensively isolated, but more openly connected with others, we would not be so intent on protection and security. We would see less need to guard knowledge or block transparency, and relaxing these provocative barriers would begin to reduce conflict. Can we even conceive of living conflict-free? What a profound difference that would make: Human beings would not be so prone to mislead themselves, to misinterpret others, or to make mistakes that create waves of worry and guilt.

Consider the effect that freedom from guilt and fear would have on our lives—we could live wholeheartedly, perhaps for the first time. The heart would not close down to the wholeness of our own being, to other beings, or to our precious earth. Our spirit would begin to expand beyond the boundaries of the isolated personal present into interconnectedness that embraced our human family, together with our shared inheritance from the past and our joint possibilities for the future. We would begin to take care of 'self' and 'other' in a definitive way, an innovative way, a knowledgeable way.

With access to knowledge that had a broader, lighter perspective, we would not be forced to inhabit a space where openness is utterly elusive,

Light of Knowledge

and time is experienced as an oppressive force. When knowledge is no longer constricted, the territories and positions of space stop manifesting solid, resistant borders that clash against each other. Barricades naturally come down, separateness and hostilities ease up. If knowledge is broadened out, then time no longer seems just a narrow strip of highway to get from here to the next job. If we penetrate the agitated waves on the surface of experience, diving deeper into time, its momentum slows and loosens up; the relentless deadline pressure that prevents enjoyment and meaningfulness is released into creativity. Rejuvenated by these new relationships with space and time, our human energy would transform readily, the divisive, frustrating, and flammable characteristics that have been endangering our world would have a chance to heal, and we ourselves would move toward wholeness and trustworthiness.

Knowledge can open borders, release positions, and unlock the tight chains of limited moments to revitalize the human spirit. Knowledge brings expansion and extension of senses, of communication, of thoughts and feelings. Knowledge knows how to regrow a stable base of caring that is not vulnerable to the fear that shuts down sharing between self and other. Knowledge can show the way to simplify complexity before it creates unbearable disorganization, confusion, and even chaos. Knowledge itself can restore the conditions that support the improvement of knowledge and guarantee wellbeing.

A Third Class of Knowledge

A third class of knowledge arises when, based on our personal experience, we acknowledge that our knowledge could be rooted deeper, could be more complete, and more effective. Recognizing that personal anxiety, pressure, and lack of control still remain despite society's great progress in knowledge, we have to admit that external improvements have not provided complete inner satisfaction. The temporary exhibition of external abundance brings limited benefits because the material realm is subject to unpredictable change and in any case will not last forever.

As we recognize these limits in our own experience, we stop demanding complete satisfaction from the material realm and begin to look elsewhere for the meaningfulness of our lives. It becomes clear that our energy has been caught up in the external side of human life—the

Light of Knowledge

pursuit of knowledge has been oriented outward, in our study of the physical realm and even in our approach to the mental realm, which relies on objectified images and conceptualized processes and structures that 'externalize' the internal. Our language, our math, our arts and sciences all depend on the descriptions of outward-directed knowledge and its subject-object structure where knowledge is treated as a tool for creating something that does not yet exist—a scientific advancement, a new artistic expression, a medical innovation, or a technological solution.

The third class of knowledge calls for the process of inner self-discovery, the making of a new partnership with mind. Mind, meaning, and spirit are resources that the modern world has not yet tapped in a truly inner inquiry. Innovative awakened light of knowledge is our best resource, our eternal friend that can foster a richer and more meaningful way of life while also transforming into wisdom that uplifts the human spirit. We already have a great deal of preparation for this new inquiry, based on the first two classes of knowledge. Yet after all the education, accomplishment, and celebration, something to explore remains, something unknown still awaits discovery. What we have been leaving out of account all this time could become the doorway opening to a new horizon. Now is the time to step through that door and engage the third class of knowledge.

A Newborn Vehicle

Introspection and self-discovery were much more prominent in ancient times when wisdom traditions fostered a holistic way of life balanced between inner and outer. The well-trained individual was neither caught up in the material world nor alienated from it. This balance is suitable for us today, for most of us do not have the choice to not participate in the external structures of society. Similarly, if we were grounded in a more comprehensive knowledge, our present knowledge would not need to be rejected, but could be put to use in creative ways for finer tangible results and more effective concrete solutions with fewer side-effects and more predictability.

To access knowledge of the third class, we must move toward dimensions unmapped in the past. We continue today to operate mind with very old patterns, faithfully carrying on programs that may be obsolete and even detrimental to our wellbeing. As we look into this mind operation more closely and internally, we begin

Light of Knowledge

to notice the defects—contradictions, projections, unfounded opinions, residues and toxicities, self-deceptions, and a pervasive unease that seem to be sure signs that the knowledge program needs a serious upgrade. It seems clear that modern mind must move beyond 'modern', beyond 'postmodern' to an entirely new model not dependent on accepting or rejecting past patterns. To take the next step along the path of knowledge, we need a newborn vehicle, newborn but parentless.

For moving in this new direction, existing concepts and words are not sufficient for they are already fixed and always fixating, and where we wish to go has not been mapped out and pinned down. That very impulse to match a new territory to the old map is part of our outdated program, and we would do well on this journey not to engage that exhausting enterprise. Likewise, the habit of automatically following thoughts, or feeling compelled to run emotional energies, keeps us entangled in the old externalized patterning, and takes us away from, rather than toward, the more inner dimensions.

If we wish to beware that programming without creating more unease, we need a very light and playful touch. To coax mind into opening up so that we can enter more deeply inside, we need

A Newborn Vehicle

to make friends with mind. Our habitual efforts at control, our longstanding demands for special experience, our clumsy poking around, trying to spy on mind—these are not beneficent gestures of friendship! Without re-agreeing to the old contract, we could make a new partnership on less rigid, more playful terms.

The old terms demand sustaining a great seriousness, guaranteeing that we know what we are doing according to mind's handed-down standards; mind then enforces these standards of rightness and wrongness with hope and fear. If a little more not-knowingness were allowed, if not-knowing were not a problem, then mind could relax its guard. So we could try on this attitude, and if mind were to respond in an unexpected friendly way, we could relax too. We might find we are dancing together differently, like partners, leading and following and leading, one mirroring the other, enjoying the mutual responsiveness that is a delightful new revelation and may point to a new understanding of dualistic dynamics.

Entering the Light of Knowledge

To explore this dynamic more deeply, we might consider what the Dharma teachings refer to as

V Ladder of Understanding

skillful means. A skillful means is not a mechanical method, such as your ordinary, everyday 'how'— how to do, how to find, how to fix. This kind of 'how' is not at all necessary for an inner inquiry. Rather, skillful means is a 'how' that is instantly and intrinsically part of knowingness itself. The very sense of identity of mind-ness or self-ness points out something not-yet understood, and that seeing-something-to-see opens up naturally, unfolding fresh new angles in an inner individualized innovation. Each sense of presentness is knowledge presenting presentations knowledge can know.

We glimpse a middle way, not an external way that relies on words and concepts. And not an internal way that fixates on a stagnant inner ground we might call emptiness, where we safely and securely settle down and hold onto the right 'being', the right 'knowing'—the right posture to protect the self. To invite mind to keep opening up, we return to the ease and honesty of not-knowing: within this thought, this feeling, without already knowing 'the right answer', we ask directly: who is labeling what, who is selling what to whom, who is being hired by whom.

Each single thought does double-pointing, from who to whom, and we need to know that

Entering the Light of Knowledge

double to understand the regime of dualistic mind. This doubling is underway always, as we practice meditation or investigative analysis, and in every moment of daily life. Does the investigator know who is investigating and who is receiving the feedback? Does the meditator know who is identifying 'emptiness'? Does the devotee recognize who is asking for help? Mind does know how to play, how to structure, how to produce. Mind makes many kinds of 'how's' and we can learn 'how' it does this. We might even dare to wonder—how else could mind have been labeled as mind, if not by mind itself.

Exercising this art of seeing and science of mind, we see that each sense of feeling, of thought, and of 'I' is inviting us into the light where, free to not-know, we can see the unseen anew any moment —the repeatedly unseen self-established ground of self-identity. Not-knowing has a profound gnosis quality that allows fresh, live knowing to rise and return to being, and being becomes knowing. This instant, intimate embrace brings our investigation so close, knowing is no longer far afield. We do not even need to settle down or set forth in pursuit of understanding. There is no time or space for a 'how' or a label, so close are we to knowledge. Innovative understanding just opens, like petals unfolding in space, responding to the light of the sun.

Learning to delight in mind's playing all the roles and playfully looking into it, we prepare ourselves to entertain a new inner perspective. Entering that perspective, we see that all the higher knowledge disciplines we have cultivated for millennia—including philosophy, science, and spiritual meditative investigation—all the thoughts and ideas must relate to and come from the 'I, me, and mind' of the researchers and believers. It is therefore more important than we usually realize to understand what has come before us in history, and what we ourselves have inherited and are faithfully following.

Let us look into 'how' our ways of thought have been mind-created, how the interactions of senses, feeling, language and concept, observation and identification become a sophisticated vehicle for transporting us both to understanding and to mis-understanding. The search engine of knowledge has the ability to work with either one creatively, so whether we receive expected old feedback or unexpected new feedback, both extend the continuum of knowledge, though in different directions, one more beneficial and accountable than the other.

Opening Time for Seeing

The Dharma texts describe skillful methods for expanding knowledge that the wisdom traditions have used for many centuries, practices of profound states of blissful samadhi where we enter into the liberating openness of space and touch the vibrant power of time with our whole being. With the right knowledge and means, awareness might unite with time so that whatever we are experiencing moment by moment, each juncture of time and knowing would allow the living point of being to expand, opening inner and outer innovative seeing.

Every single action of body, speech, and mind offers opportunity to move in this new direction into the light of knowledge. Myself as the do-er is already contacting experience of this next thought. Connecting inwardly and outwardly into being, knowledge embraces each instant and timing expand. Now mind's magical maneuvers can be penetrated with more precision, and new vistas for exploration spontaneously appear—knowing sees into the design of the rules of language, the linkages of time and space with knowing, and the mechanisms that connect senses, feelings, identities, motivations, and consciousness, and bond human being to stagnancy, fruitless repetition, and frustration. Understanding the operation of the old programs feeds back to us a new taste of knowledge, fully qualified to lead us further, conducting the human spirit into the open.

Embracing Joy

As we tap a new source of understanding and attune ourselves to inner inquiry, we understand we are not missing anything that we need. Inner and outer walls begin to crumble of their own accord when we trust that knowledge is totally available, just like sunlight. Light of knowledge is already presenting, providing, and protecting under all circumstances. Its dynamic creativity brings precision and incisiveness that clear up confusion and release a new joy of being into our lives. Its timeliness catalyzes the right relations at the right junctures so presentations and communications are well suited to each inner and outer receiver, not stale repetitions that prompt the same old feedback and reinforce the authority of the already-known.

Embracing Joy

The delicious nourishment that our being begins to receive from the taste of new inner knowledge allows a deep relaxation of grasping and paranoia, so that heart and mind stay open to the further flow of understanding. What a joy to contact this openness innovation in ourselves, for ourselves, as ourselves! Such pure creativity can be increased through devotion to the exhilarating artistry of creativity itself.

In ancient times this powerful, impressive artistry was known in India as *lila*, and in Tibet as *rolpa*. The pure aesthetic experience of all knowledge is felt as an expression of intense, instantaneous beauty. The presence of seeing-and-being-knowing allows the unfolding of the tightest corners of mind, for we discover that cooperation with the fields of light-sensing is already underway. From all the senses, aesthetic 'seeings' pour forth, inviting us deeper into the light, allowing us in, without any interference from the old border patrols of the dualistic regime.

Knowing is operating smooth and free, unrestrictedly; appearance is appearing playfully and full, with no dark corners or hidden recesses where anything could be left behind. Going in and in, closer and lighter, until to and from disappear, mind opens wide, degree after degree into light. There is no more behind or beneath, for the whole background and underground is 360 degrees wide open, a warm space of goodness that is utterly, totally reliable. Bound by no names, always available, light-filled space does not need to be captured, for it can never be lost, only ignored. When we embrace the light of knowledge, immersing ourselves in the brilliance of an all-surrounding beauty, joy takes us by the hand, and leads us unhesitatingly toward inherent freedom of knowing knowing itself. Unceasingly un-sealed—was, is, forever un-sealed.

Such freedom and goodness are not a new costume for old mind, because the worn-out hope and fear program has no role to play, the old pressure and anxiety cannot take hold for long. The tight triangle of mind operation, matter, and energy transforms to delightful magic. All the old programs and patterns can now be run playfully, joyfully, for finer purposes. Seen from this innovative perspective, those old mechanisms and structures have instructed us very well down through the centuries, giving us repeated feedback until we learn how they operate and appreciate their own distinctive transmission of the genes of knowledge. This educational journey has been accumulating momentum, allowing us to enter the light of knowledge, where the accelerating learning curve comes full circle at last.

Conducting Global Benefits

To grow more accustomed to joy and freedom in the light of knowledge, we practice harmonizing senses, feelings, identities, motivations, and consciousness; appreciating each element, resolving the conflicts, and synthesizing the different interior vibrations until we glimpse for ourselves what it might mean to embrace *lila* and learn to live with her, inhabiting a space of great beauty and ease of timing.

Then we are ready to invite family and friends to join a new dialogue, learning to communicate knowledge by embodying it to our best ability. The interplay of mind and mind grows richer and smoother, more refreshing and invigorating, released from territoriality and possessiveness, so that independent point and counterpoint in harmony becomes the new measure of success. Uplifted and emboldened by eliciting such beautiful music among friends, we would no longer hesitate to unleash new knowledge in a wider arena for the welfare of the world.

Light of Knowledge

Global knowledge in unison is neither a blending of opinions nor a cobbled together patchwork of compromises. To create such a symphony of new understanding among many parties, we rely not only on the abundant resources of the millennia that fill our knowledge treasury, but on the natural strength and expandability of knowledge itself, and on the growing ground of caring, our solidarity with all beings, which is revealed by entering into the light of knowledge and the space of goodness.

Having already observed individually and directly the old patterns of mind, we know these mechanisms and designs are much more fundamental than anyone's personal psychology. Human beings everywhere are subject to these antiquated programs, and under their domination, we are all moving in a similar direction. This global inner perspective opens up a truly innovative energy that simply could not be accessed with the old tools and technologies. On the basis of knowing our shared world to be a singular field of being, inherently connected to the space of goodness, human caring could be catalyzed to completely new heights.

Joining with 'others' in 'our one world', united in native sympathy through the similarities of mind that we share as a species, we could conduct skillful communication that makes a difference for others on the individual level, as well as on the social, educational, political, economic and other levels. The fundamental patterns of the regime of mind subject us to a similar fate wherever we live upon this earth. Viewed from the perspective of limited knowledge, this 'fate' appears fixed and full of suffering. If we listen from the global inner perspective, we could hear the same sorrowful tale from any citizen of the world. It is our tale, and we know it thoroughly, inside out:

"No matter how I try to fulfill my wishes, I have no guarantee that even my most fundamental physical, emotional, and spiritual needs will be met. This is beyond my control. Meanwhile I am forced to deal with undesirable conditions no matter how carefully I arrange my life. My time is dominated by the pursuit of happiness that tantalizes me with hope and expectations and then undermines me with anxieties and fear of loss. These repeating patterns of hope and fear that I face in my life, I see repeated and reflected in my family and society—it seems no one has any solutions. Every day is filled with an endless array of duties imposed by the structures of society. My time is packed full of tasks I can never complete, and I end most days feeling guilty. I am so busy that I have no time for simple pleasures or enjoying my nearest and dearest. This way of life does not offer much meaning. I do not see what else to do but how can I live this way?"

How indeed? Now we understand that new choices depend on a newborn knowledge, which is reborn always, extending and expanding, ready to be shared widely with our human family because the benefit of self and other have finally merged. When the subject and the object have the opportunity to reunite, then the microcosm and macrocosm no longer remain divorced but could remarry for good. Of course we still have the option to stay bonded to the old dictatorial programs—all options are open. But new knowledge gives us a choice, a taste of freedom and goodness that the human spirit might elect as its new authority, an authorless authority of light shining everywhere.

The Readiness for Knowledge

This is the right place and now is the right time for the ancient Dharma traditions to influence modern disciplines in a way more fundamental than

The Readiness for Knowledge

has yet taken place; and here, I believe, is the cutting edge of knowledge for our era. The readiness for knowledge is present. Though perfectly translated models of Buddhist thought and practice have not yet been prepared, though western professionals are not oriented toward traditional monastic ways of life, still the essence of Dharma understanding can be applied to the human mind today. Anyone who wishes to engage the philosophical ideas and meditative exercises is free to join in this endeavor. We are organizing classes and seminars to create an avenue for personal participation so that individuals can experience for themselves the enjoyment and benefits of a new kind of inquiry that stimulates the expansion of knowledge.

It is time to express what we know, to respond to our sense of obligation for the future. Knowledge illuminated by caring and love expands naturally, sustaining and protecting the precious human spirit that enlivens us all. Everyone is welcome. Come gather together with us and we can share our understanding without restriction. At Dharma College, we shall experiment and test, we shall converse and contemplate, inspiring ourselves individually and working together as teachers and students to exercise

Light of Knowledge

and refine understanding. To initiate our inquiry process, we have several texts that we trust will catalyze innovative dialogue. As that dialogue moves in productive and fruitful directions, we will have new and illuminating experience to share with a growing circle of friends and associates.

May our work together extend the light of knowledge far into the future, for the benefit of beings in all times and places.

SUSTAINING THE LIGHT

Efforts to Preserve a
1,400-year Heritage of Wisdom

In 1959, the invasion of Tibet marked the beginning of a systematic destruction of an ancient wisdom tradition that had been protected in this remote Himalayan land for more than fourteen hundred years.

Tarthang Tulku, educated in Tibet at the feet of the greatest masters of the 20th century, was in India before this process began. From Tibet, he had followed his root guru 'Jam-dbyangs mKhyen-brtse'i Chos-kyi Blo-gros to Sikkim to receive teachings. For some time he had practiced on retreat in Bhutan, but after his teacher's passing from life, he went on pilgrimage to honor his master's memory. As he traveled, tens of thousands of Tibetans fled their homeland, abandoning all but their most precious possessions—the books and art that were the very foundation of their culture. Almost overnight, Tibet was taken over by a foreign power that sealed its borders, closing off all avenues of travel and communication. Those who had escaped found themselves refugees in foreign lands, struggling to survive, cut off from home, family and all that gave meaning and structure to their lives.

Unable to return to Tibet, Tarthang Tulku lived amongst the refugees, where he witnessed the human and cultural cost of this devastation first-hand. In 1962, when the Indian government offered fellowships at Sanskrit University in Benares to representatives of the four Tibetan schools, at the request of the head of the Nyingma school, he accepted the position designated for his tradition. In Benares, his research into the transmission of Buddhism from India to Tibet clarified how strongly and for how long the lineages and teachings stemming directly from the Buddha had flowed into Tibet. With them had come many treasures of India's cultural heritage—literature, art, philosophy, and medical sciences nurtured for centuries within India's monastic universities.

Shortly thereafter, Tarthang Rinpoche became the Dalai Lama's representative to the World Conference on Religion held in Mysore, where he met a wide range of scholars from eastern and western universities. Then, determined to preserve all he could of a heritage so valuable yet faced with irrevocable loss, he returned to Benares, where he established Dharma Mudranalaya, a press named for the printing house in Derge famed for its production of sacred texts. After 6½ years, he left India to continue his work in America. In Europe, he met with supporters who urged him to stay, but he continued on to America and arrived in Berkeley, California in 1969.

By 1975, he had incorporated the Tibetan Nyingma Meditation Center (TNMC), re-founded Dharma Publishing in Berkeley, initiated relief efforts for refugees in India and Nepal, established the Nyingma Institute, and become an American citizen. That same year, he founded Odiyan on the open crest of California's central-northwestern coast. In 1976, he incorporated Nyingma Centers and charged it with guiding and protecting the growth of the new organizations. In the next few decades, as these founding activities expanded internationally, he went on to establish more than twenty additional organizations in the U.S., Asia, Europe, and South America. (*See below*, p. 417)

Under his guidance, Dharma Publishing developed skills and printing capacities in the process of producing more than a hundred titles ranging from translations of key traditional texts and overviews of Buddhist history and teachings to Rinpoche's books related to mind and finding balance in work and daily life. Books produced by Dharma Publishing sustained the educational programs of the

Nyingma Institutes developing abroad and laid the foundation for major preservation projects. As early as 1981, although he lacked Tibetan editors and researchers, he directed a small staff of Western students in producing the sDe-dge edition of the complete Tibetan Canon, a compilation of over 5,000 texts in 120 atlas-sized Western volumes, and followed it a few years later with an 8-volume catalogue/bibliography.

In 1983, after years devoted to teaching, writing, and publishing books in English, Rinpoche created the Yeshe De Text Preservation Project and broadened efforts to obtain and publish sacred texts, including those never before compiled into collections. In 1986, he delegated responsibility for daily operations to senior students he had trained and focused on a preparing series of even more comprehensive publishing projects, beginning with *Great Treasures of Ancient Teachings*. (*See below*, p. 409)

In 1989, to establish the means for distributing books to Tibetan centers in India and bordering lands, Tarthang Rinpoche founded the Monlam Chenmo (World Peace Ceremony) an annual gathering regularly attended by more than ten thousand monastics and laypersons. For the past 24 years, participants have assembled in

Sustaining the Light

Bodh Gaya, site of the Buddha's enlightenment, to receive books filled with teachings empowered by over twenty-six centuries of research, meditation, and realization. More than four million books, three million sacred art reproductions, and thousands of prayer wheels have since been distributed freely, on a non-sectarian basis, to representatives of more than 3,000 Tibetan centers in Asia. In 1995, the Longchen Varna, a major ceremony commemorating the Parinirvāṇa of the great Nyingma master Longchenpa, was revitalized and observed in Sarnāth. Held shortly after the Monlam Chenmo, this ceremony was relocated to Bodh Gayā in 2002 to enable more Monlam participants to attend.

In 2004, with TNMC's encouragement and support, the Theravādin sanghas of Sri Lanka and Southeast Asia returned to Bodh Gayā after a hiatus of 800 years. This first international Tipiṭaka chanting ceremony, an auspicious event of historical significance, marked a reunion of the main streams of the Buddhist Sangha. Every year, leaders of the Sangha, monks, and laypersons from nine countries have assembled at the Bodhi Tree in ever-increasing numbers to recite Suttas and prayers from the Pāli Tipiṭaka.

Sustaining the Light

TNMC's efforts to revitalize the holy places as active centers for pilgrimage and devotion have continued in Bodh Gayā and at other significant sites. These include repairs and renovations of temples and stupas, the creation of gardens, and the installation of fourteen Triratna bells at sacred sites in India, Sikkim, Nepal, Sri Lanka, China, and Burma. Bearing prayers and mantras, these massive bells symbolize the presence of the Buddha and commemorate the teachings.

The Monlams, the bells, the prayer wheels, commemorative plaques and other projects that restore awareness of the sacred are Rinpoche's way of expressing the cultural aspects of Buddhism. Although increasing costs stretch TNMC's capacities beyond their limits, the long-range value of this work merits extraordinary efforts, and TNMC wishes to continue.

To this end, the Head Lama has established four Light Foundations charged with supporting important ceremonies and lineages, the vitality of sacred sites, the education of monks and nuns, and the creation of temples, stupas, libraries, and places of retreat in significant locations. More recently, he has founded Mangalam Research Center and Dharma College in Berkeley.

Sustaining the Light

In the midst of these activities, the Head Lama has worked for 38 years to build Odiyan into a place where the treasures of Tibetan culture could be safely preserved and displayed for the benefit of future generations. Five temples, nine libraries, and an Enlightenment Stupa—all repositoriies of sacred art and teachings—exemplify the proportions and forms of Buddhist architecture, Relevant to every aspect of experience, forms expressing profound realization can inform the dialogue between eastern and western ways of understanding and sustain the transmission of the deepest meanings inherent in the Buddha's teachings. Nature participates equally: Three decades of cultivation have enabled Odiyan's forested groves and gardens to convey the harmonious balance that sustains the realms of nature and human being. In anticipation of the 38th annniversary of Odiyan's founding, residents have been refreshing them by planting hundreds more trees in great variety.

Tarthang Rinpoche's activities are far-reaching in scope and application; the intensity and focus necessary to sustain them are difficult to describe. But mindful of the stresses of modern Western lifestyles, from time to time he expresses his thoughts in books that can be translated and widely shared. Nearly six years in preparation, this latest book, *Revelations of Mind,* is offered to relieve misunderstandings that embroil us in confusion and free the mind to operate in ways that promote health and happiness.

In releasing this book for publication, the author has said, "Our mind is the creator of all we experience, yet we suffer, for we do not understand the creator or the creation. But if we can closely contact the processes by which mind generates experience, we can give ease to our mind and appreciate the true nature of our embodiment. We can make our mind our best friend and our most reliable companion."

44 Years of Production
Dharma Publishing Books in Tibetan

5 PUBLICATIONS OF THE BKA'-'GYUR

sDe-dge	T	poti	120
sDe-dge	T	Western	133
sTog Palace	M	poti	112
sNar-thang	M	poti	102
Nyingma Edition (sDe-dge)	M	Western	36

4 PUBLICATIONS OF THE BSTAN-'GYUR

Nyingma Edition (sDe-dge)	M	Western	92
sDe-dge	T	Western	275
sNar-thang	M	poti	225
Selections from sDe-dge bsTan-'gyur	T	poti	107

ADDITIONAL PUBLICATIONS

Great Treasures of Ancient Teachings	M	Western	637
dKar-chag (Jewel Lamp)			2
rNying-rgyud rGyas-pa	T	poti	149
dKar-chag			2
Bodh Gayā vols (Tibetan commentaries in addition to bsTan-'gyur)	T	poti	382

TOTAL BKA'-'GYUR AND BSTAN-'GYUR VOLUMES	1202
GRAND TOTAL (ALL VOLUMES)	2374

T = typeset
M = manuscript (facsimile)
Mostly distributed

Dharma Publishing Books in English

Translation Series

SŪTRAS (Direct teachings of the Buddha)

1983 Voice of the Buddha (Lalitavistara Sūtra)
1985 Dhammapada (Essential Topics)
1986 The Fortunate Aeon (Bhadrakalpika Sūtra)
1986 Wisdom of Buddha (Saṁdhinirmocana Sūtra)
2002 Gathering the Meanings: Arthaviniscaya Sūtra

ŚĀSTRAS (Works by Indian and Tibetan Masters)

1973 Calm and Clear (Lama Mi-pham)
1973 Legend of the Great Stupa (Padmasambhava)
1975-76 Kindly Bent to Ease Us (Longchenpa)
1975 Mind in Buddhist Psychology (Asanga, Yeshe Gyaltsen)
1975 Golden Zephyr, Nāgārjuna's Letter to a Friend, (Nāgārjuna, Lama Mipham) 1975
1977 Elegant Sayings (Nāgārjuna, Sakya Pandita)
1978 Life and Liberation of Padmasambhava
1979 Buddha's Lions: Abhayadatta's Lives of India's 84 Great Siddhas
1983 The Marvelous Companion, The Beauty of Compassion (Āryaśūra's Jātakamālā)
1983 Mother of Knowledge: The Life of Ye-shes mTsho-rgyal
1987 Master of Wisdom (Nāgārjuna)

Selected Books

1987 *Leaves of the Heaven Tree*
       (Kṣemendra, Padma Chöphel)
1987 *Joy for the World* (Candragomin)
1995 *Path of Heroes: Birth of Enlightenment*
       (Zhechen Gyaltsab)
1999 *Invitation to Enlightenment*
       (Letters of Mātṛceṭa and Candragomin)
2007 *Now That I Come to Die* (Longchenpa)
2009 *Padmasambhava Comes to Tibet*

Crystal Mirror Series: Surveys of Buddhist Civilization, directed and edited by Tarthang Tulku

1969-1974 1-3 *Footsteps on the Diamond Path* Fundamental Vajrayana teachings and their application to daily life. German, Portuguese

1975 4 *Bringing the Teachings Alive* Biographies of Guru Padmasambhava and his twenty-five disciples, with 2 works by Longchenpa Portuguese

1977 5 *Lineage of Diamond Light* Introduction to the Buddha, Dharma, and Sangha and the Mahayana schools of India and Tibet.

1984 6 *Roots of Transmission* Mahayana schools and philosophical traditions of India and Tibet. Dutch, German, Portuguese

1984 7 *Buddha, Dharma, and Sangha* The life of the Buddha, the unfolding of the Dharma, and the growth of the Sangha in the context of world history.

Selected Books

1992 8 *Light of Liberation* Buddhism in India from the origin of the Śākyas to the twelfth century
Portuguese

1994 9 *Holy Places of the Buddha* Guide to the eight central places of pilgrimage in India. *Czech*

1996 10 *The Buddha and His Teachings* The path and qualities of the Perfect Buddhas, the life of the Buddha Śākyamuni, and openings of the Sūtras preserved in the Tibetan Canon.

1996 11 *Masters of the Nyingma Lineage* Accounts of more than 350 masters of the Nyingma tradition of Tibetan Buddhism, from teachers active at the time of the Buddha to the gTer-ma masters of the Tibetan traditions.

1997 12 *The Stupa: Sacred Symbol of Enlightenment* Forms of the Buddhist stupa, significance of sacred architecture, and the benefits of circumambulation.

BOOKS BY TARTHANG TULKU

Nyingma Psychology Series

1977 *Gesture of Balance* Fundamental teachings on awareness, self-healing, and meditation.
Chinese, Czech, Dutch, French, German, Italian, Japanese, Korean, Polish, Portuguese, Thai, Spanish, Vietnamese

1978 *Openness Mind* Advanced presentations on mind and meditation.
Czech, Dutch, French, German, Italian, Korean, Portuguese, Spanish

Selected Books

1978 *Kum Nye Relaxation* Stress-relieving exercises based on the Tibetan medical system.
Bulgarian, Chinese, Czech, Estonian, French, German, Hungarian, Italian, Japanese, Latvian, Polish, Portuguese, Russian, Spanish

1978 *Skillful Means: Patterns for Success* A new philosophy of work that empowers individuals to build meaning into daily life.
Czech, Dutch, French, German, Hungarian, Italian, Portuguese, Spanish, Swedish, Vietnamese, Thai

1981 *Hidden Mind of Freedom* Topics and practices for cultivating mind's vital energy and developing confidence in the spiritual path.
Czech, Dutch, French, German, Italian, Japanese, Portuguese, Spanish

1984 *Knowledge of Freedom: Time to Change* Investigating habitual patterns of mind and questioning fundamantal assumptions,
Dutch, German, Portuguese, Spanish

1987 *Ways of Work* Experiences with the Skillful Means approach to work and spiritual practice.

1994 *Mastering Successful Work* Establishing structures for accomplishment, transforming unproductive attitudes, attaining success in daily life, and advancing on spiritual path.
Czech, Dutch, French, German, Italian, Portuguese, Spanish

1998 *Teachings from the Heart* Essays on Meditation, Turning to the Dharma, and other facets of Western interest in Buddhism,
German, Portuguese, Spanish

Selected Books

2002 *Mind over Matter* Reflections on traditional and Western views of Dharma study and practice.
Dutch, German, Portuguese, Spanish

2005 *Milking the Painted Cow* Teachings on facets of 'Illusion Mind'.

2005 *Joy of Being.* Advanced practices explore Kum Nye's application to the senses, the perceptual process, and cognition. *Czech, German, Portuguese*

2012 *Kum Nye Dancing* Exercises that introduce the mind to the treasures the body offers.

2013 *Revelations of Mind* A new way of understanding self, mind, and experience.

Time Space, and Knowledge Series

1977 *Time, Space, and Knowledge* A new vision of reality based on fundamental elements of experience.
Dutch, German, and Italian

1987 *Love of Knowledge* Experiential exercises, graphics, poetry, and logic that stimulate creativity and open new ways of knowing. *Dutch and Portuguese*

1990 *Knowledge of Time and Space* Celebrates the power of time and space to free mind from limitations.
Portuguese

1994 *Dynamics of Time and Space* Perspectives that open mind to new dimensions of experience.

1997 *Sacred Dimensions of Time and Space* Inquiry into space as the source of experience and time as the hidden source of meaning.

Selected Books

Restoring the Cultural Heritage of Tibet

1972 *Sacred Art of Tibet*   Beauty as a manifestation of the ultimate and significance of deities as guides to perfection.

1993-1995 *The World Peace Ceremony: Prayers at Holy Places*   4 vols. Description and photographic record of the founding of the Monlam Chenmo.

1992 *From the Roof of the World*   Unique photographic memorial of Tibetan refugees entering India in 1959 and early efforts to stabilize their culture.

2001 *Your Friends the Tibetan Refugees*   A chronicle of projects developed by the Head Lama and implemented by the Tibetan Aid Project.

2006 *Is Tibet Forgotten?*   Tarthang Rinpoche's account of the Tibetan diaspora and 36 years of efforts to help refugees reestablish the foundations of their culture.

2010 *The Triratna World Peace Bell*   Gift and installation of 14 ten-ton peace bells to holy places in India, Nepal, Sri Lanka, Sikkim, and China.

Nyingma Activities in the West

1975-2008 *Annals of the Nyingma Lineage in the West*   Inside details of Tarthang Tulku's work in the West from 1969 through 2008 (39 years).

1993 *Ways of Enlightenment. Education at the Nyingma Institute.* Topics of knowledge inspired by Lama Mi-pham's encyclopedic "Gateway to Expertise" (mKhas-'jug). *Portuguese*

Selected Books

1998 *Enlightenment is a Choice*   45 essays on facets of Buddhist philosophy and practice.

Healing Power of Nature

1991 *Mandala Gardens*   Shaping a mandala of trees and flowers to reflect the diversity of cultures and the power of nature to uplift mind and spirit.

2008 *Garland of Flowers*   A meditative journey into realms of natural beauty.

2010 *Seeing the Beauty of Being*   Thoughts on the relationship of mind and nature, expressed in the photographic context of the groves, gardens, birds, and animal life of Odiyan.

2012 *Lotus Mandala: Sacred Garden*   Gardening as a path to understanding, inspired by the gardens of Odiyan.

Books for Children

Twenty-six illustrated adaptations from traditional Jatakas instill respect for life and the value of patience and generosity. Additional books for children include *Treasury of Wise Action* for young readers and three illustrated books that introduce episodes of the Gesar epic.

ORGANIZATIONS AND PROJECTS ESTABLISHED BY TNMC

Tibetan Nyingma Meditation Center (1969) Center of the Nyingma Mandala, established as a corporation sole. Headquarters of the Head Lama, director of TNMC projects and organizations.

Dharma Mudranalaya (1970, incorp. 1975) DBA Dharma Publishing. Preserves the literature, art, and sacred texts of the Buddhist tradition; introduces this heritage to the West through publications in English and promotes their translation.

Nyingma Institute (1972) Introduces the study and practice of Tibetan Buddhism to America and provides a forum for East-West interactions.

Tibetan Nyingma Relief Foundation (1969, incorp. 1974) Founded to provide humanitarian and cultural support for Tibetans in exile. As the Tibetan Aid Project (TAP), sponsors the production of sacred texts prepared by the Yeshe De Project and their shipment to the World Peace Ceremonies for distribution.

Odiyan (1975) Operates under the Head Lama of TNMC. Houses extensive libraries of sacred texts and art. Envisioned as a center for the study and practice of Buddhism, translation, research, and the creation of sacred art.

Nyingma Centers (1976) Guides the development of programs and projects of the international Nyingma centers in Europe and Brazil.

Organizations and Projects

Yeshe De Project (1983) Promotes research into Tibetan Buddhist civilization; fosters the preservation and translation of sacred texts.

Tarthang Monastery Reconstruction Project (1983) Initiated to help rebuild Tarthang monastery in eastern Tibet and support traditional study and practice.

Dharmacakra Press (1988) Prints Yeshe De religious texts at Ratna Ling for distribution to Tibetan centers in Asia.

Center for Creative Inquiry (2000) Established independently as a vehicle for exploring the Head Lama's Time-Space-Knowledge vision: its implications and applications.

Light of Buddhadharma Foundation International (LBDFI) (2002) Serves to restore, beautify, and reactivate the holy places of the Buddha; supports ceremonies for the purpose of reviving Buddhism in Asia.

Ratna Ling Retreat Center (2004) Offers retreats and programs on body-mind integration and healing; the home of Dharma Mudranalaya.

Nyingma Trust (2008) Established to protect the health and safety of the Nyingma community of Dharma practitioners and support their commitment to TNMC's projects.

Mangalam Research Center (2009) Researches terminology of Buddhist texts and supports making Western languages into vehicles for the Dharma; develops data base and tools for translators.

Organizations and Projects

Guna Foundation (2009) Founded to share the accomplishments of the TNMC mandala with the world, and to ensure that treasures of the Tibetan culture survive long into the future.

Dharma College (2010) Offers classes and programs in accord with its founding vision, to introduce and teach worldwide a new way of understanding and healing mind.

Nyingma Association of Mandala Organizations (NAMO) (2012) Supports and protects the activities of the Nyingma organizations.

****

INTERNATIONAL NYINGMA CENTERS Founded by TNMC to extend the teaching, spiritual practice, artistic, publishing, and aid activities of the mandala established in the U.S. 4 established to date:

Nyingma Centrum Nederland (1989) Amsterdam

Nyingma Zentrum Deutschland (1989) Cologne

Instituto Nyingma do Brasil (1989) São Paulo

Associação Cultural do Grupo Nyingma do Rio (1996) Rio de Janeiro

****

INTERNATIONALLY-ORIENTED FOUNDATIONS AND PROJECTS ESTABLISHED BY TNMC

Bodhgaya Trust (1993) Established to continue the World Peace Ceremony at Bodh Gayā

419

Organizations and Projects

Nyingma Buddhist Trust (1993) Provides ongoing support for the continuation of the lineages and practices of the Nyingma school of Tibetan Buddhism.

Longchen Varna Project (1995) Initiated to commemorate the enlightened activities of the great Nyingma master Kun-mkhyen Klong-chen-pa and take inspiration from his life and teachings.

Triratna Peace Bell Project (2002) Funds the casting of 5-foot bronze bells bearing prayers and mantras and their installation at holy places in commemoration of the Buddha's teachings of universal harmony and peace. 14 installed to date.

Mangalam Light Foundation (2005) Reviews, approves, and funds projects proposed by LBDFI and the other Light foundations.

Ananda Light Foundation (2005) Established to support the practice of sādhanas and pūjas and similar religious and spiritual activities.

Prajna Light Foundation (2005) Established to further the education of Tibetan practitioners and provide opportunities for practice.

Vajra Light Foundation (2005) Established to ensure the survival of bKa'-ma and gTer-ma traditions and support the lineages of Tibetan Buddhism.

Sarnath International Nyingma Institute (2006) Established in India to provide courses in English, Pali, Sanskrit, Tibetan, and Dharma studies.